THE TREATY OF
GUADALUPE HIDALGO, 1848

PAPERS OF THE SESQUICENTENNIAL SYMPOSIUM,

1848-1998

SPONSORED BY THE DOÑA ANA COUNTY HISTORICAL SOCIETY
LAS CRUCES, NEW MEXICO

FEBRUARY 28, 1998

Introduction by

LOUIS R. SADLER

John Porter Bloom, Editor

Doña Ana County Historical Society

and Yucca Tree Press

First Printing   1999

Doña Ana County Historical Society

THE TREATY OF GUADALUPE HIDALGO, 1848
        1. Southwest United States - History.   2. United States-Mexico Border History.
        3. U.S.-Mexican War - 1846-1848.
        I. Richard Griswold del Castillo.   II. John Grassham.   III. Mark J. Stegmaier.
        IV. Malcolm Ebright.   V. Deena J. Gonzales.   VI. Josefina Zoraida Vásquez.
        VII. Louis R. Sadler

Library of Congress Catalog Card Number: 99-67403
ISBN: 1-881325-39-3

Cover: Original fresco by Frederico M. Vigil; photograph by Murrae Haynes and Michael O'Shaughnessy; design by Stephen Matson

Editor's Note

The Doña Ana County Historical Society sponsored the symposium at which the essays in this volume were first presented. This Sesquicentennial Symposium to commemorate the Treaty of Guadalupe Hidalgo, 1848-1998, took place in Las Cruces, New Mexico, on February 28, 1998, at the Las Cruces Hilton, with an attendance of 262 persons chiefly from New Mexico and west Texas. This event was supported in part by a grant from the New Mexico Endowment for the Humanities.

Robert Himmerich y Valencia, emeritus professor of history, University of New Mexico and editor, *New Mexico Historical Review*, supported the present publication in several ways, particularly in helping arrange use here of the magnificent mural by Frederico Vigil. Señor Vigil painted the mural in the Santa Fé County Courthouse in commemoration of the war of 1846-1848 and the Treaty by which it was concluded, and graciously provided the reproduction on our cover. Additional very valuable support was provided by the Department of History, New Mexico State University, and the Río Grande Historical Collections, NMSU Library. Music of the period was provided by Professor Jon Linford, Music Department, NMSU; and first-rate entertainment in the evening by the *Mariachi de Oñate* of Oñate High School, Las Cruces.

This symposium followed one equally successful in 1996 by the Doña Ana County Historical Society in commemoration of "New Mexico's Year of Destiny, 1846." The papers presented then were published informally by the society in a volume now out of print.

The Symposium Planning Committee was co-chaired by Janie Matson, incoming society president, and the undersigned. Outstanding service was rendered to the committee by Madeleine Vessel as secretary and Robert Pick as treasurer. The other members, who all contributed in very important ways, were Clarence Fielder, immediate past society president, Randy Fischer and Martin Gemoets. Special appreciation is due to Beverley Pirtle for handling the sales table during the symposium. At the table and working in many other ways were other society-member volunteers too numerous to list here, without whom the event could not have succeeded.

John Porter Bloom

Las Cruces, New Mexico

TABLE OF CONTENTS

LIST OF ILLUSTRATIONS

Photographs

Maps

INTRODUCTION
Louis R. Sadler

One spring afternoon ten years ago, I sat in the governor's conference room in the Round-house in Santa Fé for a meeting with the new United States Ambassador to Mexico, John D. Negroponte. I was there by invitation, presumably because of my specialization in Mexican history, and I had organized the sixth annual meeting of United States-Mexican Border Governors in Las Cruces the previous year, and I had served as chair and vice-chair of the New Mexico Border Commission throughout the 1980s.

Ambassador Negroponte's visit was principally ceremonial, to touch base with the governors of the four American states which border on Mexico. Before the conference got underway I chatted briefly with him, inquiring about some high officials in Washington whom I had gotten to know during the previous year's Border Governors' conference.

The governor opened the affair by welcoming the ambassador and introducing the persons at the large, circular conference table—principally members of his cabinet. Ambassador Negroponte explained briefly that he was present because the U.S.-Mexican border was becoming increasingly important and he wished to listen to the governor and his staff as to problems that existed and how he might help. The usual litany of problems were then put forward—illegal immigration, drug smuggling, etc.

As the brief meeting wound down, one of the governor's ranking cabinet members, who shall remain nameless, inquired rather plaintively, "Why don't Mexicans like us?" Knowing that I was a Mexican specialist, the ambassador asked me to respond. I did so in the most elementary way, describing the U.S.-Mexican War, its causes, and the resulting Treaty of Guadalupe Hidalgo. It was as if the cabinet member had never heard of any of it and, although he did not say so, he conveyed the feeling that he wondered, "what does any of this have to do with the question I asked?"

The ambassador rolled his eyes as I attempted to explain to the cabinet secretary why indeed Mexico did not love the United States. I am not sure if I succeeded. But that particular interchange has stuck with me over the last decade. The cabinet secretary was not a fool or an idiot. He was a college graduate—but thank goodness had never been in any of my classes. He simply did not know or had never learned about something called the Treaty of Guadalupe Hidalgo.

One does not have to be a historian in American diplomacy to know that there are a number of famous treaties to which the United States is a signatory, and one famous one (the 1919 Versailles Treaty) to which the U.S. Senate refused to consent. These include the Treaty of Paris (actually there are two by this name, one in 1783 that ended the American Revolution, one in 1898 that ended our war with Spain), and of course the 1790s Jay's Treaty and Pinckney's Treaty. And then there is the Treaty of Ghent, named for the town in Belgium where negotiations between the United States and Great Britain ended the War of 1812.

There is a small point to be made here because most students are unaware why treaties are named for certain places. It is both customary and traditional for the name of the site of the treaty negotiations to be given to the treaty. Thus the obscure village north of Mexico City— Guadalupe Hidalgo—in September 1847 was where negotiations started between an American diplomat, Nicholas P. Trist, and a most reluctant team of Mexican representatives. The result was the Treaty of Guadalupe Hidalgo, which brought the U.S.-Mexican War to an end.

In some respects, at least geographically speaking, it is America's most important treaty. It was this treaty, after all, by which the United States acquired its two most populous states, Texas (which had really been lost already, but to which Mexico now gave up all claim) and California, in addition to what constitutes now the states of New Mexico, Arizona, Nevada, and portions of Colorado and Utah. In toto, Mexico lost almost half of its national territory.

So this treaty, which the former New Mexico cabinet secretary knew nothing about, is the subject of this edited volume of papers.

It is to the enormous great credit of a county historical society—specifically the Doña Ana County Historical Society—that we owe a well attended conference in Las Cruces, New Mexico, in which a number of first-rate historical papers were presented on the 150th anniversary of the treaty. With this volume these papers are now preserved for posterity. We also hope that they will be read and remembered.

The Department of History at New Mexico State University is delighted to have played a small role in this conference and in the publication of these proceedings. The driving force behind it was John Porter Bloom, to whom we are all indebted.

Finally, we can only hope that the unnamed cabinet secretary and those who have followed him, now and in the future, will read with interest the events surrounding the Treaty of Guadalupe Hidalgo and why it is really important today, still, in relations between Mexico, New Mexico, and the United States of America.

RICHARD GRISWOLD DEL CASTILLO

Ricardo, a name he is pleased to use often, Griswold del Castillo served as an appropriate anchor for the symposium which has provided the essays for the present volume. His scholarly monograph published in 1990, then and still the only such study devoted solely to the Treaty of Guadalupe Hidalgo, was well known to all participants in the symposium. He was much in demand in this sesquicentennial year of 1998, at borderland conferences and several lecture series in which the U.S.-Mexican War of 1846-1848 was commemorated. Still, the essay below calls our attention to particular aspects of the treaty and its inheritance which reach beyond his previous writings. It is a rich area for study.

With a name appropriately suggesting a bicultural inheritance, Griswold del Castillo was drawn in graduate studies to social history, especially Chicano social history. His doctoral dissertation at the University of California, Los Angeles, led to his first major publication, *The Los Angeles Barrio, 1850-1890: A Social History* (1980), which was well received and established him as an esteemed player in this field of history which came into prominence in the 1970s. He provided "the first detailed analysis of the changes that transformed one of the most important Mexican pueblos in the Southwest into a Chicano urban barrio." He showed that Mexican-Americans were not only a rural but also an urban people, and thus he contributed positively to our understanding of the roots of Mexican-American culture in the borderlands.

This success was followed by many others. In 1984, taking a broader scope, the University of Notre Dame Press published his *La Familia: Chicano Families in the Urban Southwest, 1848 to the Present*, also very well received in scholastic and popular circles. In his 1990 treatise on the Treaty of Guadalupe Hidalgo, Griswold del Castillo used broad strokes to describe not only the diplomatic processes involved in concluding the treaty but especially the treaty's long-standing, socially significant implications. His writing resonated with awareness of the importance, just then being fully recognized in scholarly circles, of racial and ethnic prejudice in the history of U.S. foreign policy. But his approach is consistently balanced and fair, innocent of the too-common "presentism" found in some writings whose authors apply 1990s standards to 19th-century personalities.

More recent books have also been well received: *Chicano Social and Political History in the Nineteenth Century* (ed. with Manuel Hidalgo) in 1992; *César Chávez: A Triumph of Spirit* (with Richard García) in 1995; *North to Aztlan: Mexican Americans in United States History* (with Arnoldo de Leon) in 1996; and in the same year, published by the Centro de Investigación Sobre los Estados Unidos of the Universidad Nacional Autónomo de México, *Aztlan Reocupada: A Political and Cultural History since 1945—The Influence of Mexico on Mexican American Society in Post-War*

1

America. His writing is consistently marked by clarity joined with scholarly thoroughness, and his research is notable for its depth and originality. These features are reflected very felicitously in his lectures and other oral presentations.

Richard Griswold del Castillo's consistent success in publication of books, articles and scholarly reviews has been paralleled and perhaps challenged by his active participation in teaching, consulting and civic activities. At this writing he is acting director of the Master's Program in Liberal Arts and Professor of Mexican American Studies, San Diego State University. His consulting activities have drawn him to California State University, Fullerton; to KERA-TV, Dallas; to Instituto Mora, México, D.F.; to the universities of Arizona and Monterrey, Nuevo Leon, México; to the Rockefeller Foundation; and elsewhere.

Locally in southern California, he has been very active also, for instance on the City of San Diego's Historical Sites Board and the Board of Directors, Centro Cultural de la Raza of San Diego. He is working on several projects relating to art history, one being a team-taught course using Chicano Park (San Diego) as an iconographical introduction to themes in Mexican and Chicano history. This is part of a larger effort to organize a conference on the park as a community historical event. He is married, father of six and grandfather of five to date.

John Porter Bloom
Las Cruces, New Mexico

THE TREATY OF GUADALUPE HIDALGO AND NEW MEXICO:

BORDERS, BOUNDARIES AND LIMITS

Richard Griswold del Castillo

The Treaty of Guadalupe Hidalgo is the document that ended the Mexican-American War of 1846-1848, and the oldest treaty still in force between the two countries. This agreement, now 150 years old, has been important in shaping international and domestic history. My purpose here is to discuss the boundaries set up by the treaty and how they continue even now to influence social and political life in the United States. I will focus on two kinds of boundaries, internal and international. By internal I mean the land boundary issue as it was worked out after 1848. As many Americans know, the land issue is very much alive today in New Mexico and also alive and well in Texas, but pretty much a dead issue in California. The issue of international boundaries may appear to have been settled but the treaty actually created new boundary problems that are with us today, as we shall see.

International Boundaries

International boundary questions raised by the Treaty of Guadalupe Hidalgo have a complex history. Article IV of the treaty attempted to define the geographic boundaries between the United States and Mexico. The problems in defining the land boundary running between El Paso and San Diego became a source of controversy almost immediately after ratification of the treaty, leading to the negotiation of the Gadsden Treaty in 1853. The other portion of the boundary described by the Treaty of Guadalupe Hidalgo, the Río Grande, also became a source of conflict between the two countries, largely because of periodic changes in the river's course caused by flooding and accretion.

In July 1849 representatives of each country met in San Diego to begin the task of marking the international boundary on the ground. A year later they finished tracing and marking the line between Upper and Lower (Baja) California. When the commissioners then met in El Paso to begin surveying the boundary between the New Mexico Territory and the Mexican states of Chihuahua and Sonora, they discovered that there were serious geographical errors in the original map that had been used by the negotiators of the treaty. The map cited in the treaty, an edition of Disturnell's map of North America, located the town of El Paso del Norte (now Ciudad Juárez) about thirty miles northeast of its true location. If the map were to be followed literally, the rich Mesilla Valley and the Santa Rita del Cobre mines would remain in Mexican territory.[1] This was clearly unacceptable to the expansionist Democrats in congress who wanted to open the mineral wealth of and to build a suitable transcontinental railroad through the region. The American member of the commission, John Russell Bartlett, and the Mexican member, General Pedro García-Conde, argued over the issue. Eventually both agreed that the defective Disturnell map should be used to set only the southern boundary of New Mexico. There were enough discrepancies in the map favoring the U.S. position that the Mexican commissioner agreed to a compromise. This line gave the Americans a railroad route and the Mexicans possession of the mining district. The U.S. Congress refused, however, to accept this agreement.

In 1852 the situation in the controversial Mesilla strip became explosive as Mexican repatriates and Anglo-Texan and New Mexican cattle ranchers moved into the area. The governor of Chihuahua claimed jurisdiction and the governor of New Mexico Territory threatened to occupy the area with force. Further provocation came when American troops occupied the Mexican communities of Ysleta, Socorro, and San Elizario, below El Paso, claiming that changes in the course of the Río Grande now made them part of the United States. In 1848 these three communities comprising almost six thousand people had been on the Mexican side of the river.[2] This volatile situation, along with the desires of key members of the American congress for rights of transit across the Isthmus of Tehuantepec and a release from the obligations of Article XI of the Treaty of Guadalupe Hidalgo, led in 1853 to the dispatch of a new American Minister to Mexico, James Gadsden. After conversations between President Antonio López de Santa Anna and Gadsden, and threats of military force from Washington, Mexico signed the Gadsden Treaty or, as known in Mexico, El Tratado de Mesilla. As eventually modified by the American congress, the United States agree to pay $10 million and Mexico ceded the territory the Americans wanted for a railroad while allowing abrogation of Article XI on the Treaty of Guadalupe Hidalgo and granting rights of transit across the Isthmus of Tehuantepec to the United States. The new treaty also granted the United States an additional 29,142,000 acres of Mexican territory and released it from the obligation of policing Indians of the border area. And it may well have prevented the renewal of warfare between the two nations.

The most significant conflict arising from the 1848 treaty boundary involved an area of land known as the Chamizal, a 600-acre tract that eventually became part of downtown El Paso, Texas. El Chamizal, so named for a kind of bush that flourished there, had been located south of the Río Grande and thus was part of Mexico in 1848. By 1896, because of flooding and resultant changes in

---

[1] For the primary reports of the boundary survey from the American point of view see John Russell Bartlett, "Report on the United States and Mexican Boundary Commission," House Executive Documents, 34th Cong., 1st sess. (Serial no. 861). Recent research using the Mexican Archives has begun to unfold the Mexican side of the story. See Joseph Richard Werne, "Mexico's Interpretation of the Guadalupe Hidalgo Line," (paper presented before the American Historical Association annual meeting, Washington, DC, 1987). See also Harry P. Hewitt, "The Treaty of Guadalupe Hidalgo Revisited: Myths and Realities of the Mexican Boundary Survey," (paper presented same time and place).

[2] Angela Moyano Pahissa, *México y Estados Unidos: Orígenes de una relación, 1819-1846* (México, DF: Secretaria de Educación Pública, 1985), pp. 175-177. Pahissa believes that the transfer of these three communities after 1848 was a violation of Article V of the treaty specifying boundaries.

the river's course, the tract was situated north of the river and was claimed to belong to the United States. For some 115 years the City of El Paso, the State of Texas, and the U.S. government asserted jurisdiction over this section of land. In this they were challenged consistently by the Mexican government.

The Chamizal controversy was a source of diplomatic tension between the two countries, and as such it proved to be the impetus for the establishment of a convention of November 12, 1884, to establish rules to determine the political status of "banco" lands, *i.e.*, land areas that were transferred from one side of the river to the other through changes in the river channel. Five years after the convention was established the countries jointly set up an International Boundary Commission with representatives from both Mexico and the United States, to have the responsibility of settling any further disputes involving river and land boundaries. After detailed engineering studies the joint commission would recommend transfers of banco lands to either Mexico or the United States as dictated by circumstances.

On November 14, 1895, the Mexican government tested the Mexican-American agreements flowing from the Treaty of Guadalupe Hidalgo by submitting for adjudication by the International Boundary Commission a tract of land within the Chamizal zone.[3] The commission heard arguments from both sides but was unable to reach agreement. The case was finally submitted to an Arbitration Tribunal (a specially enlarged session of the International Boundary Commission) in 1911 with the prior understanding that both countries would abide by the decision. A major argument for the Mexican case involved reference to the original Treaty of Guadalupe Hidalgo boundary line, which stipulated that the United States was acquiring lands lying north of the Río Grande in 1848. The tribunal's decision was to divide the tract, giving a portion to Mexico and leaving the rest with the United States. This decision leaned heavily on the language and intent of the original Treaty of Guadalupe Hidalgo.[4] The U.S. government, however, refused to accept the results of this arbitration decision, arguing that the river's changed course was not caused by slow accretion as had been maintained by the Mexican government, but had happened due to violent flooding. Under the 1884 convention regulating banco lands, both countries had agreed that violent changes in the river bed would not be considered legitimate changes in the boundary. The American negotiator, Anson Mills, held that the arbitration decision was so vague and indeterminate that it was impossible to execute.[5]

For the next fifty years the dispute was a continuous irritation in relations between the two countries. Various proposed solutions were advanced and rejected. The unstable political climate in Mexico during the 1910 revolution and the American delay in diplomatic recognition made an early settlement impossible. One effect of this controversy was to create uncertainty about land titles in the Chamizal zone, and as a result the area degenerated into a slum.[6]

---

[3] J.J. Bowden, *The Ponce de Leon Land Grant*, Southwestern Studies Monograph no. 24 (El Paso: Texas Western Press, 1969), pp. 31-33.

[4] Lic. Joaquin D. Casasus, *El Chámizal: Demanda, réplica, alegato é informes* (Mexico, DF: Eusebio Gómez de la Puente, 1911), pp. 4, 568-569, 583. Those who served on the tribunal were Eugene Lafleur (France), Anson Mills (U.S.), and F.B. Pulga (Mexico).

[5] *Ibid.*, p. 616. See also Berta Ulloa, *La revolución intervenida: relaciónes diplomáticas entre México y los Estados Unidos (1910-1914)* (México, DF: Colegio de México, 1971), pp. 260-262.

[6] Bowden, *Ponce de Leon Grant*, pp. 38-39.

President John F. Kennedy in 1963 responded to suggestions from the Mexican government that the issue could be laid to rest, and as a result a settlement was reached finally along the lines of the 1911 arbitration award.[7]

The Mexican reaction to the Chamizal issue illustrated the depth of feeling it had aroused. Here for the first time since 1848, Mexico was reclaiming part of its national domain from the United States. In Mexico there was a tremendous emotional reaction. President Adolfo López de Mateos and President Lyndon B. Johnson met in El Paso and both spoke of how this act signified a new era in U.S.-Mexican cooperation and brotherhood. The ceremonies of transfer were carried live on Mexican television to more than 75 million people. September 24 was declared Chamizal Day in both Ciudad Juárez and El Paso. Candlelight parades were held; *corridos* were composed; and a massive fiesta was celebrated.[8]

For Mexicans the Chamizal agreement had a rich meaning: it was a symbol of the persistent efforts of Mexico to rectify past injustices, of the emerging international strength of Mexico, of the triumph of the rule of law and peaceful negotiation, of the political strength of the ruling party (PRI), and a vindication of an independent Mexican foreign polity. Leopoldo Zea, a leading Latin American philosopher, in a lengthy editorial interpreted the end of the Chamizal conflict as a triumph of Mexican dignity over force of arms. He added:

> It was not the result of a Machiavellian net but more the clear and natural expression of an old Mexican tradition. And the result was that this pride, far from hurting the country, strengthened and helped it. Within the same terrain of prideful dignity, it was possible to grant concessions where politics and power would have failed.[9]

Mexican diplomatic victories over "the colossus of the north" have been rare in historic relations between the two countries. Negotiations involving the international boundary have resulted more often in lengthy, complex exchanges and compromises. An example of this has been the issue of international territorial waters. Due to political pressures for control over oil exploration and fishing grounds, the extent of the offshore territorial claims of Mexico had important economic implications. For many years the Mexican government cited the Treaty of Guadalupe Hidalgo as the authority for a claim of nine miles of territorial waters. Article V in the 1848 treaty stated that "the boundary line between the two Republics shall commence in the Gulf of Mexico, three leagues from land, opposite the mouth of the Río Grande." A league in the Spanish period was variously defined but it was generally accepted to be approximately three miles. The specific language on this point in the Treaty of Guadalupe Hidalgo was inserted by the American diplomat, Nicholas Trist, borrowing from a Texas Boundary Act dated December 19, 1836, where the offshore territorial waters were claimed to run "three leagues from land, to the mouth of the Rio Grande." Ironically a Mexican

---

[7] Sheldon B. Liss, *A Century of Disagreement: The Chamizal Conflict, 1864-1964* (Washington, DC: University Press of Washington, 1965), Appendices A and B for texts of Conventions and Statistics.

[8] See Antonio Luna Arroyo, ed., *México recibe El Chámizal* (México, DF: Editorial Justa, 1964), for an account of the media reaction to the Chamizal ceremonies.

[9] *Ibid. Novedades* (México, DF), Sept. 29, 1964.

counter proposal to the original treaty language had omitted this proposed three-league stipulation.[10]

As previously noted, in a lawsuit by Texas in 1960, the Treaty of Guadalupe Hidalgo was cited as an authority for that state's claim to offshore oil lands (*U.S. v. Louisiana et al*. 363 U.S. 1 [1960]). The Mexican government followed this case very carefully because its outcome would either support or damage Mexico's claim to expanded offshore fishing and oil exploration territory. In 1961 Alfonso García Robles chaired the Mexican delegation to the Second United Nations Conference on the Law of the Seas and presented an extensive argument in favor of Mexico's claim to a territorial sea larger than the then conventional three-mile limit, citing and interpreting the Treaty of Guadalupe Hidalgo extensively. He presented historical evidence to show that the U.S. government itself, in diplomatic despatches, considered the three-league provision valid. On April 30, 1848, the British government sent a note to the United States protesting the language of Article V of the treaty since it violated their understanding of U.S. territorial waters (one league or three miles). Secretary of State James Buchanan wrote in reply that "the stipulation in the treaty can only affect the rights of Mexico and the United States" and that "the government of the United States never intended by this stipulation to question the rights that Great Britain or any other power may possess under the laws of nations."[11] Thus the U.S. government recognized in 1848 that its maritime boundary with Mexico extended three leagues from shore but that this provision was not binding on third parties and did not necessarily extend each country's offshore territorial possession to a line three leagues out. In the Gadsden Treaty of 1853 this same three-league or nine nautical miles limit was reconfirmed. In 1935 Mexico by an act of its congress fixed nine nautical miles as the breadth of its offshore waters. The U.S. government, however, did not then accept Mexico's claimed limit.

The American side of the argument was presented by Arthur H. Dean, president of the American Society of International Law. He argued, in the 1961 Law of the Seas Conference, that the much cited case of *U.S. v. Louisiana et.al*. applied only to relations between Texas and the U.S. government, not to foreign countries. The Supreme Court, Dean argued, refused to consider any issue of territorial seas in its review of the 1848 treaty as it applied to this domestic case. Moreover the Treaty of Guadalupe Hidalgo was silent regarding a territorial sea boundary on the Pacific Ocean and this seemed to substantiate the view that the negotiators were not primarily interested in this issue in delineating the international boundary.[12]

On December 26, 1969, after years of discussion between the United States and Mexico over the meaning of Article V with respect to territorial waters, both countries finally agreed to a twelve-mile limit. This ultimate resolution relied to some degree on the historical interpretation of existing international treaties, especially the Treaty of Guadalupe Hidalgo. The agreement was spelled out in a formal treaty signed in Mexico City on November 23, 1970, and ratified in 1971 by the United

---

[10] "Notes and Comments," *American Journal of International Law*, Vol. 55, No. 3 (July 1961), pp. 669-679.

[11] Karl M. Schmitt, "The Problem of Maritime Boundaries in U.S.-Mexican Relations," *Natural Resources Journal,* Vol. 22 (Jan. 1982), pp. 138-153.

[12] For a summary of the Robles-Dean debate see Alberto Szekey, *México y el derecho internacional del mar* (México, DF: Universidad Nacional Autónomo de México, 1979), pp. 85-87.

States This 1971 comprehensive treaty also resolved long-standing problems arising from the Colorado River and Río Grande boundaries.[13] By this new treaty, Article V of the Treaty of Guadalupe Hidalgo was formally terminated along with Article I of the Gadsden Treaty. In its place was set forth a new provision for a twelve-mile offshore limit and also a Pacific territorial sea boundary.

Internal Boundaries: The Land Issue

First the issue of land boundaries in New Mexico. In 1848 private and communal land grants in New Mexico covered about fifteen million square miles. In order to determine the federal domain, congress established the Office of Surveyor General, to which broad powers were accorded. In August 1854 congress appointed a Surveyor General for New Mexico Territory. Once in Santa Fé, he had considerable trouble getting the Hispano land-grant owners to file their claims with his office. As a result, only twenty-five town and private claims and seventeen Pueblo Indian grants had been confirmed by congress by 1863. One thousand claims had been filed by 1880, but only 150 had been acted upon by the federal government.[14] As the number of unconfirmed grants in litigation before the Surveyor General and congress lengthened, so too did the legal expenses incurred by Hispano pueblos and ranchers. Such lawyers and politicians as Stephen Benton Elkins and Thomas Benton Catron formed the nucleus of the Santa Fé Ring, a confederation of opportunists who used the long legal battles over land grants to acquire empires extending over millions of acres. The most famous example of the land-grabbing activities of the Ring was the manipulation of the Maxwell Land Grant, a Spanish claim of 97,000 acres that became inflated through the actions of the Ring to a final patent of 1,714,074 acres.[15]

Besides losing their lands to rapacious lawyers and politicians, Hispanos suffered from changing whims in national politics. In 1885 the newly elected Democratic president, Grover Cleveland, removed the Republican Surveyor General of New Mexico and replaced him with his own appointee, William Andrew Sparks. Historian Ralph Emerson Twitchell described Sparks as being "steeped in prejudice against New Mexico, its people and their property rights."[16] The new Surveyor General decided that his Republican predecessor had been corrupt and had given away far too much federal land, and therefore his decisions and those of congress regarding land should be reviewed. In the name of reform Sparks revoked the approval of twenty-three grants. This process of reviewing New Mexico claims gave no assurance that the Treaty of Guadalupe Hidalgo, or indeed the rule of law, would outweigh the political influence of persons behind the scenes.

---

[13] U.S. Department of State, *Treaty with Mexico Resolving Boundary Differences ... November 23, 1970* (Washington, DC: G.P.O., 1971).

[14] New Mexico land-grant litigation, a complex subject, can be treated only superficially in a survey such as this. For a more detailed analysis of the legal and historical aspects involved, see Victor Westphall, *The Public Domain in New Mexico: 1854-1891* (Albuquerque: University of New Mexico Press, 1965); J.J. Bowden, *Spanish and Mexican Land Grants in the Chihuahuan Acquisition* (El Paso: Texas Western Press, 1971); and Ralph Emerson Twitchell, *The Leading Facts of New Mexican History* (Albuquerque: Horn & Wallace, 1963, reprint), Vol. 2, pp. 458-461.

[15] Howard Roberts Lamar, *The Far Southwest, 1846-1912: A Territorial History* (New York: Norton, 1966), pp. 141-146.

[16] Twitchell, *Leading Facts*, Vol. 2, p. 462.

When Benjamin Harrison became president in 1889, federal land policies in New Mexico would change again. Under pressure from developers and New Mexico Hispanos, congress in 1890 began to consider legislation that would settle the outstanding land claims. Railroad interests wanted to have the full extent of the public domain established, so that they could get federal grants. Hispano landholders in New Mexico sought to speed up the land-confirmation process and to reverse previously adverse rulings. Writing to Matías Romero, the Mexican Minister Plenipotentiary to the United States in 1890, the predominantly Hispano Commercial Club of Las Vegas laid out their complaints. They urged Romero to use his influence to secure passage of a new land law:

> The American government has thus far, though over 40 years have elapsed, neglected to provide a competent court to pass on the validity of the claims of those who were once Mexican citizens .... We, with great respect petition you to champion the cause of our people and again represent to the State Department at Washington the evil inflicted on us by the failure of the U.S. government to fulfill in this respect its obligations incurred by the Treaty of Guadalupe Hidalgo.[17]

For its part, the Mexican government followed the proposed legislation with interest but was unable, for diplomatic reasons, to advocate the Hispano cause in congress. The Mexican government did instruct Romero to react to court cases when it appeared that there was prejudice against former Mexican citizens in the application of the law, once it went into effect. Romero, for his part, suggested that his government publicize its concern for its former citizens so that they would be better able to oppose unjust actions taken against them in violation of the Treaty of Guadalupe Hidalgo.[18]

On March 3, 1891, the president signed into law a bill to establish a Court of Private Land Claims. The Treaty of Guadalupe Hidalgo was invoked specifically as a guiding document for this court, although wording in the act provided that it would apply only to "persons who became citizens by reason of the Treaty of Guadalupe Hidalgo and who have been in the actual adverse possession of tracts not to exceed 160 acres."[19] The court was made up of five judges plus an attorney representing the interest of the U.S. government. Unlike the California Land Commission, the New Mexico Court of Land Claims did not require those holding perfect titles to apply to the court for confirmation—only those who had not fulfilled all the regulations of Spanish and Mexican law. Those not presenting their claims within two years would be considered to have abandoned their grants. The law also restricted to eleven square leagues (about thirty-six square miles) the amount of land that would be allowed for a communal or town grant and stipulated that errors in previous decisions by congress would be indemnified at not more than $1.25 per acre.

Meeting in Denver, Colorado, and Santa Fé, New Mexico, between 1891 and 1904, the New Mexico court operated by the strict rule that confirmation of a land grant required proof that the

---

[17] Commercial Club, Las Vegas, NM, to Matias Romero, Minister Plenipotentiary, Dec. 27, 1890. Archivo de Secretaría de Relaciónes Exteriores (A.S.R.E.), no. 11-5-1.

[18] Matias Romero to Secretaría de Relaciones Exteriores, A.S.R.E., *ibid.*

[19] *Analysis of the Act to Establish a Court of Private Land Claims*, A.S.R.E., *ibid.*, p. 309.

Spanish or Mexican granting official possessed legal authority for any action at issue. There had been a good deal of confusion in New Mexico's political history, therefore many grants were held not to be legitimate because of the alleged "illegitimacy" of the Mexican governing authorities.[20] The court also was very strict regarding what it considered a proper survey, documentation, and full compliance with every Mexican law regarding land tenure. As a result of this less-than-liberal interpretation of Spanish and Mexican laws, the court in New Mexico rejected two-thirds of the claims presented before it. Ultimately only eighty-two grants received congressional confirmation. This represented only six percent of the total area sought by land claimants. Thus, using the Court of Private Land Claims, the federal government enlarged the national domain at the expense of many Hispano villages, leaving a bitter legacy that would fester through the next century. The land issue would explode in 1963 with Reies Tijerina and the formation of La Alianza Federal de Mercedes Libres, and again in the 1980s with the Flores land-grant case, centered also in Tierra Amarilla, New Mexico.

Texas

In Texas the land issue has an equally tortured history. In 1856 the U.S. Supreme Court ruled that the Treaty of Guadalupe Hidalgo did not apply to Texas. Nevertheless the treaty did figure into the negotiation of a later international agreement. In 1923 Mexico sought recognition for its new, revolutionary government and conducted a series of meetings called the Bucareli Conference. It was during this conference that the issue of the status of land grants in Texas and the applicability of the Treaty of Guadalupe Hidalgo resurfaced. This conference was convened to settle outstanding claims of both countries and to pave the way for U.S. diplomatic recognition of Mexico's government.

To counter U.S. claims for damages suffered by Americans during the 1910 revolution, the Mexican government decided to present the claims of its former citizens in the American Southwest. Initially they presented 836 claims amounting to $245 million. Almost $193 million of this amount was for Texas land claims invalidated in violation of the Treaty of Guadalupe Hidalgo.[21] The Mexican government, through its consulates in Texas, actively solicited land claims from heirs of original land-grant owners who had been dispossessed of their lands after 1848. Increased Anglo-American migration into South Texas after 1848 had led to a large number of these claims. This was the area of Texas in which the first battles of the Mexican-American War had occurred and where there had been much diplomatic disagreement prior to the war. Many Tejano grants in this region were perfected Spanish claims that had been recognized by the Mexican government. Many Tejanos who had lost title to their ancestral lands after 1848 had their cases presented on their behalf by the Mexican government during the Bucareli negotiations.

On September 8, 1923, the United States and Mexico agreed to establish a commission to review Texas land grants. Eventually 433 cases, valued at $121 million, were presented on behalf of

---

[20] Ralph Rowley, "The Acquisition of the Spanish Borderlands: Problems and Legacy" (Ph.D. dissertation, University of New Mexico, 1975), p. 210.

[21] *State v. Gallardo et al.*, 135 S.W. 664, "Juridical Decisions Involving Questions of International Law," *American Journal of International Law,* Vol. 6 (1912), p. 227.

heirs. In 1941, after much delay, the Texas land claims were settled on the international level with the Mexican government assuming the obligation of compensating the Texas heirs. The issue was not resolved in fact, however, for while both the United States and Mexico recognized the legitimacy of the Texas claims under the Treaty of Guadalupe Hidalgo, the Mexican government refused to carry out its financial obligations—this despite constant pressure from the Tejano land-grant heirs.[22]

In Conclusion

In the first half-century after ratification of the Treaty of Guadalupe Hidalgo, hundreds of state, territorial and federal legal bodies produced a complex tapestry of conflicting opinions and decisions. The property rights of former Mexican citizens in New Mexico and Texas proved to be fragile. Within a generation the Mexican Americans who had been under the ostensible protections of the treaty became a disenfranchised, poverty-stricken minority. The promises of the treaty remained just that.

The boundaries, both international and domestic, that were the subject of the Treaty of Guadalupe Hidalgo proved to be as fluid and changing as the Río Grande. Still, the treaty refuses to go the way of other paper accords, such as the Louisiana Purchase Treaty or the Florida Treaty. This is because its constituents, the Hispanos, Mexican Americans and Native Americans of the Southwest have not allowed it to become an antiquarian artifact. The contemporary issues of Mexican immigration, drug smuggling, and foreign economic competition are all affected in indirect ways by this agreement reached in 1848. A growing "Hispanic" minority within the United States will compel us in years to come to consider, again and again, the meaning of the Treaty of Guadalupe Hidalgo within American history.

---

[22] Rudolfo O. de la Garza and Karl Schmitt, "Texas Land Grants and Chicano-Mexican Relations: A Case Study," *Latin American Research Review,* Vol. 21 (1986), pp. 123-138.

JOHN GRASSHAM

John Grassham's roots run deep in New Mexico's soil. He is a native of Albuquerque, and his ancestor, Charles H. Beaubien, was one of the first French-Canadians to settle in New Mexico after Mexican independence in 1821. At an early age, Grassham developed a passion for his family's history, which led him to the broader study of western American history.

As an undergraduate at Eastern New Mexico University, Grassham worked as a student archivist in the Golden Library. During this time he encountered New Mexico's State Historian, Dr. Myra Ellen Jenkins, Grassham's friend and mentor until her untimely death in 1993. After graduating from ENMU, Grassham worked as an archivist with Jenkins at the State Records Center and Archives in Santa Fé. In 1983 he obtained a master's degree in history at New Mexico State University, writing a well received thesis entitled "Charles H. Beaubien, 1800-1864."

Thereafter Grassham was employed in several history-related positions. He spent two years at NMSU administering grants that supported exploration of water resources in New Mexico. He served another two years as Curator of History at the Branigan Cultural Center in Las Cruces. Between 1989 and 1991 he was employed as Photo-archivist in the Museum of Albuquerque, and then became program director for Research and Reference Services in the Center for Southwest Research, University of New Mexico.

Since 1993 Grassham has been back at the Museum of Albuquerque as Curator of History. In this capacity he has overseen a number of important exhibitions, including one in 1996 entitled "Drawing the Borderline, Artist-Explorers of the U.S.-Mexico Boundary Survey." The catalog for this exhibit is truly a work of art, including thirty-five color plates and more than fifty-five black-and-white sketches and drawings. According to the catalog's forward, co-authored by Grassham, this was "the first exhibition ever compiled in New Mexico on the visual images completed by the U.S.-Mexico Boundary Survey."

In his paper below, "The United States-Mexican Boundary Commission," Grassham surveys the controversies surrounding the survey of the international boundary, as mandated by the Treaty of Guadalupe Hidalgo. The history of this survey is filled with drama, tragedy and political intrigue. Grassham provides informative vignettes of the men in charge of the survey, indulging an extended look at U.S. Boundary Commissioner John Russell Bartlett, a talented artist and bibliophile but an inexperienced diplomat. Grassham also presents background for Bartlett's counterpart, Pedro García Conde of Mexico. As Grassham points out, the U.S. Congress failed to approve their work, setting the stage for further controversy between Mexico and the United States. Not until 1856, after Mexico had lost even more territory to the United States with the Gadsden Purchase, was the international boundary line finally mapped. The story, as told by Grassham, reminds us of the complex issues that continued to trouble U.S.-Mexican relations following the 1846-1848 war.

Darlis A. Miller
New Mexico State University

THE UNITED STATES-MEXICO BOUNDARY COMMISSION

John Grassham

As the ink dried on the last signature finalizing the Treaty of Guadalupe Hidalgo, ending the United States-Mexican War of 1846-1848, each nation was authorized to establish an international boundary commission. Working together, the commissions were to carry out the labor-intensive task of determining the exact location of, and placing monument markers on the ground for, the official boundary between the United States and Mexico.[1] This was not going to be an easy assignment. First and foremost, the Disturnell map used as the official reference by both nations included several cartographic miscalculations.[2] In addition, none of the U.S. commissioner-designates possessed the essential credentials and competency for the vital, difficult job before them. American civilian and military personnel selected to carry out significant assignments on the survey continually quarreled over who was in charge. Mexico, on the other hand, appointed their commissioner and survey party promptly and with little difficulty. The leaders of the Mexican group had appropriate credentials and were extremely competent.

Pressure came to bear on President James K. Polk to get the American boundary commission moving ahead. Ambrose H. Sevier, longtime Polk supporter and former U.S. senator from Arkansas, obtained the presidential nod. Sevier's unexpected and untimely death interrupted his confirmation hearing, however, and the president then named John B. Weller, a one-term congressman from Ohio, to head the commission. Weller lived through the congressional hearings and was eventually confirmed owing primarily, it seemed, to his loyal party service. Unfortunately, he did not have the expertise to perform the necessary tasks. Lacking the background of many of his subordinates, Weller offered neither inspiration nor direction to the host of civilian and military personnel attached to the commission. Other problems plagued the survey party that were simply out of his control.[3]

Most of the difficulties occurred when civilian positions were designated to exercise command over military personnel assigned to the commission by the U.S. Army Corps of Topographical Engineers. Personnel problems escalated even to open conflict when civilians were placed in charge over the military. On the other hand, many times no one seemed to be in charge.

---

[1] *The Treaty between the United States and Mexico....* 30th Congress, 1st session, Senate Executive Document 52 (1848), pp. 43-47.

[2] Carl I. Wheat, "Mapping the American West, 1540-1857," in *Proceedings of the American Antiquarian Society,* Vol. 64 (1954); Lawrence Martin, *Disturnell's Map* (Washington, DC, 1937).

[3] William H. Goetzmann, *Army Exploration in the American West, 1803-1863* (New Haven: Yale University Press, 1965), pp. 157-158; and Robert V. Hine, *Bartlett's West: Drawing the Mexican Boundary* (New Haven: Yale University Press, 1968), pp. 3-4.

The individual who should have been placed in command, one of the most competent participants on the boundary commission, was Lieutenant William H. Emory.[4] He was assigned to be chief astronomer and escort commander. Like several other commission members, Emory was a West Point graduate. His nomination for the survey came through John C. Calhoun, Polk's secretary of war. A number of Emory's friends were major players in U.S. history, including Henry Clay and Jefferson Davis. His wife's great-grandfather was Ben Franklin, and other family relations included Vice President George Dallas. Not only was Emory skilled and experienced but he was also very well connected.[5]

The official surveyor appointment, also by Polk, went to a southerner and now Texas resident, Andrew B. Gray. Surveyor Gray found himself making vital decisions while lacking both knowledge and experience. Other less vital posts included medical personnel, a quartermaster, and a draftsman. Some rank-and-file positions were those of carpenter, laundress, interpreter, and at least four servants; and some insignificant jobs went to brothers of Weller and Emory. The total U.S.-Mexico Boundary Survey Commission roster contained 143 names. Given its mission, it was, in all, a large and cumbersome organization.[6]

Mexico's commission was led by General Pedro García Conde, a former military commander of Chihuahua and a noted leader. García Conde was prepared to do his best to retain for Mexico as much land as he could. One of the others on this commission was Felipe de Iturbide (son of the first and only Mexican emperor, Agustin de Iturbide) who served as Mexican official interpreter and translator. The official Mexican surveyor post was given to José Sálazar Ylarregui. Mexico's commission contained four engineers, an escort of soldiers, and a few other assistants. It was a much smaller and more manageable commission than that of the United States. Additionally, Mexican authorities assigned clear governance and leadership responsibilities within their commission.[7]

The U.S. commission was to meet with the Mexican commission in San Diego, California, in late May 1849. The American commission members chose many different routes to get to San Diego and most did not arrive as planned. Apparently the Mexican commission had the same problem, finally assembling in San Diego on July 3.[8]

With both commissions finally in place, Weller and García Conde established a base near San Diego and started to get ready for the formidable task ahead. One of their first discussions was on dealing with the problems of the Disturnell map. It was sorely flawed. Cartographer John Disturnell in 1846 had copied a map printed in 1828 which contained several errors. The imprecise calculations on the map produced immense difficulties as the commissioners tried to establish key reference points for marking the boundary line. [9]

---

[4] Goetzmann, *Army Exploration,* p. 158; Hine, *Bartlett's West,* p. 4.
[5] Goetzmann, *Army Exploration,* p. 129.
[6] Hine, *Bartlett's West,* pp. 11-12.
[7] Goetzmann, *Army Exploration,* p. 160.
[8] *Ibid.*
[9] *Ibid.*, p. 162; John Mack Faragher, "North, South and West: Sectional Countroversies and the U.S.-Mexico Boundary Survey," in Gray Sweeney and Johm Grassham, eds., *Drawing the Borderline: Artist-Explorers of the United States Bounday Survey* (Albuquerque: The Albuquerque Museum, 1997), p. 9.

Finally, on July 7, 1849, a year and five months after the signing of the Treaty of Guadalupe Hidalgo, the U.S.-Mexico Boundary Commission began its exhausting task. But the members still had more bumps than successes yet on their way. Because of the delays, for example, both commissioners faced serious cash flow difficulties. The U.S. commission had the added inconvenience of men abandoning the survey party to try their luck at searching for gold. The California gold rush also complicated severely the availability of supplies for the commission. All the while, often contradictory temperaments of military and civilian personnel continued to make progress uncertain. A particular question arose about the differing understandings between the two countries as to how long a marine league was. After much debate U.S. Surveyor Gray and Mexican Surveyor Salazar Ylarregui compromised on an arbitrary length. [10]

García Conde naturally wanted the port of San Diego for Mexico and Weller was adamant that it would be a part of the United States. Weller finally won, negotiating successfully for the line to run south of San Diego. With tenuous negotiations also came complicated geographic problems. Much of the terrain near San Diego was unbelievably difficult to survey and therefore it was very difficult to carry out the treaty provisions. [11]

As Polk's one-term presidency came to a close Weller worried about his status with the next administration. He was sure he would be continued in the senior position since he felt he was doing a fine job. Unfortunately, events on the job had little to do with his keeping the position. The troubled commissioner continued to haggle over the boundary with García Conde while his enemies in Washington pushed for his removal. With a new president in the White House, a Whig, Weller's worries became reality. [12]

When President Zachary Taylor appointed John C. Frémont as the new commissioner on June 20, 1849, the former frontier guide intended to serve in the position just long enough to clear his name for current, difficult treason trials. However, he soon received the tender of a better federal post. Upon California achieving statehood, California leaders offered him the opportunity to be their first U.S. senator. Rumors ran rampant around San Diego about Weller's dismissal. This caused a serious problem for the work. Weller could not issue requisitions on commission funds in numerous cases since many local merchants believed that he was no longer in charge of the project. Frémont carried Weller's dismissal papers with him to California but failed to deliver them to the lame-duck commissioner. Lieutenant Emory again hoped to get the appointment but his connections did not come through, and he felt insulted by the lack of support for the deserved (he believed) appointment. Surveyor Gray continued as lead surveyor, continuing also his poor relationship with the army personnel. Finally, Weller's anxious moments were over when he received word that a new commissioner had been appointed by President Taylor. [13]

García Conde and his staff were affected by all this confusion and uncertainty. They were ready to move forward. The western part of the boundary line was finished, but every delay on continuing

[10] Goetzmann, *Army Exploration*, p. 162.
[11] *Ibid.*, p. 163.
[12] *Ibid.*, p. 164.
[13] *Ibid.*, pp. 163-166.

further cost them money they did not have. At long last a new date was set to begin again: both commissioners would meet in El Paso del Norte (present Ciudad Juárez) on the first Monday of November 1850. [14] But not so fast! By that date Weller was gone, Frémont was back in Washington, and the commission was again without leadership.

When President Taylor appointed John Russell Bartlett as the fourth U.S.-Mexico Boundary Commissioner bright hopes came to the languishing commission. Bartlett was born October 23, 1805, in Rhode Island, but lived most of his early life in Canada where he clerked in his father's store. Later he held various other commonplace jobs. Displaying lifelong restlessness, he moved to New York City in 1836 where he opened a book store. He obtained a prestigious address on the street floor of the Astor House and specialized in literature and science. Bartlett's patrons included such notables as 84-year-old Albert Gallatin who was a frequent visitor in 1845, and there was also John Lloyd Stephens, known for fascinating work on Mayan ruins. Other notables included poets such as Edgar Allen Poe, artists like Henry Pratt, and many others. Bartlett's fascination with American usage of the English language developed into his perhaps most notable book, *A Dictionary of Americanisms* (New York, 1849). He also published on several other topics, notably *The Progress of Ethnology, An Account of Recent Archaeological, Philological and Geographical Researches in Various Parts of the Globe....* (New York, 1847). He held memberships in various organizations such as the New-York Historical Society, the prestigious Providence Athenaeum, and the Franklin Society. In 1848 Brown University awarded him an honorary Master of Arts degree, not a small thing since he had enjoyed no formal education. Bartlett had arrived. But yet, he was restless and still not satisfied with life. [15]

Bartlett yearned for a diplomatic post such as many of his friends had received. He envied Stephens and Ephraim G. Squier who, on foreign service duty, had pursued research projects in Guatemala. Really, Bartlett thought he wanted something a little tamer than a Latin American post. Something like ambassador to Denmark would be more his forte. However, he was informed there was nothing for him in Scandinavia. He would just have to wait. [16]

Finally, Bartlett was approached to head the boundary commission. It paid handsomely, some $3,000 per annum, quite a large sum compared to his income as a book dealer. Bartlett's innate inquisitiveness got the best of him and he agreed to take the position. Others were in nomination also, but Bartlett won with support from Stephen A. Douglas, Thomas Hart Benton, and John C. Calhoun. His prospects were not diminished by the fact that his brother-in-law was editor of the biggest newspaper in Rhode Island and governor of that state. Since he had no background in engineering he was recognized for his work in science. Adopting the role of scientist, Bartlett won senate confirmation in June 1850. [17]

Staffing the commission proved to be something of a challenge for Bartlett. Gray was retained as surveyor and Emory was brought back on board. The total number hired was twice what Weller

---

[14] Ibid., p. 168; Hine, Bartlett's West, p. 18; Faragher, "North, South," p. 7.
[15] Goetzmann, Army Exploration, pp. 167-168; Hine, Bartlett's West, pp. 7, 19-20.
[16] Hine, Bartlett's West, pp. 19-20.
[17] Ibid., pp. 11, 18-19; Goetzmann, Army Exploration, pp. 168-169.

had started out with, 283. Bartlett felt that it was extremely difficult to find the right people, and he suffered especially through the political hires. In a third-person mode, he wrote that: "with the hiring just about completed Bartlett set sail for Corpus Christy, Texas where his large party set forth. After several months of overland travel Bartlett and the surveying parties found their way to El Paso."[18]

When Bartlett arrived in El Paso he found the cost of replenishing his supplies to be exorbitantly high. Local merchants viewed the commission as a source of quick profits during otherwise slow economic times. Once the commission members had settled in, Bartlett toured the area surrounding El Paso. He learned that his Mexican counterpart had been delayed in Chihuahua. This welcome opportunity allowed Bartlett to sightsee and enjoy several dinner parties thrown in his honor. [19]

Upon García Conde's arrival, he and Bartlett met twice a week to discuss schedules and plans for continuing the survey. In the process, the men became friends and frequently dined together, enjoying each other's company. The meetings became less and less frequent, however, after the survey work began in earnest. [20]

The size of the U.S. commission was so great that no single community could accommodate them and they were spread out over several places at and near El Paso. The quartermaster and commissary were assigned to Socorro, and Lt. Col. John McClellan, Topographical Engineer officer, was placed some six miles further south at San Elizario. Lieutenant Amiel M. Whipple, an outstanding scientist-officer assisting Emory, and the surveyor camped out at the river. Bartlett stayed with James Magoffin, Santa Fé trader and merchant, resident of what would one day become El Paso, Texas. It has been suggested that both men were known revelers and given to late-night partying. All of this plus the distance from each other helped ease some tensions. However, ongoing problems within the already fractionalized group continued to fester. Throughout all the rest of the survey, resignations and terminations were a common occurrence. And departed commission personnel frequently made their negative feelings about Bartlett felt in Washington. [21]

One of the especially important appointments to the commission was that of artist. Several artists came and went before one stayed with the job. Henry Cheever Pratt, born in 1803, was a member of a pioneering group of American landscape painters that included such well known artists as Thomas Cole and Asher B. Durand, but it was Samuel F.B. Morse, portrait artist and inventor of the telegraph, who first stumbled upon Pratt and his work in New Hampshire about 1817. Pratt apprenticed under Morse, helping him complete his celebrated painting of congress. Pratt later situated himself in Boston and became a well known portrait artist. Among his early commissions was a portrait of Albert Gallatin, which suggests a possible relationship with John Russell Bartlett. By the mid-1840s, inspired by the success enjoyed by Cole, Pratt was confident enough to broaden his

---

[18] John Russell Bartlett, *Personal Narrative of Explorations and Incidents in Texas, New Mexico, California, Sonora and Chihuahua, 1850-1853.* 2 Vols. (Chicago: Rio Grande Press, 1965; orig. pub. 1855).

[19] Hine, *Bartlett's West*, p. 23.

[20] Goetzmann, *Army Exploration*, p. 173.

[21] Hine, *Bartlett's West,* pp. 23, 82.

practice. He continued to produce portraits while also exhibiting landscapes and historical and allegorical subjects. [22]

In 1851 Pratt was invited by Bartlett to join the boundary survey as its official artist. Pratt was delighted to associate himself with the project, even bringing along his son John. Pratt spent two years drawing, sketching and painting many scenes along the route. His production of paintings of the American southwest, exhibited in Boston in 1855, New York in 1858, and again in Boston in 1872, provided easterners with images that complemented and augmented Bartlett's popular book on the survey, cited above. [23]

With the survey team at last in place, the U.S.-Mexico Boundary Commission was ready to begin its work. After yet another meeting of Bartlett and García Conde with two dissimilar versions of Disturnell's map in hand, they set out in earnest on the arduous task of placing the first marker on the boundary line. [24]

The treaty called for the initial point to be where the Río Grande meets the southern boundary of New Mexico, north of El Paso. But El Paso was found to be off some 34 miles from the latitude shown on Disturnell's map, and the river some 130 miles east in longitude. Bartlett wrote on April 24, 1851, that:

> The day having arrived upon which it was agreed that the Initial Point, where the southern boundary of New Mexico intersects the Rio Grande, should be established, the document signed, and the point marked, it seems proper that I should briefly relate the history of this important portion of my duties as Commissioner under the 5th Article of the Treaty of Guadalupe Hidalgo.

Bartlett went on to describe the boundary problems in clear terms. He wrote that there were:

> ... two gross errors in the [Disturnell] map to which the Commissioners were confined by the treaty. It was discovered that the Rio Grande was laid down on this map, more than two degrees too far to the eastward—the river, where it is intersected by the southern boundary of New Mexico, being really in 106° 40' west longitude, instead of 104° 40'. [25]

García Conde was fanatic about following the latitude and longitude and would not budge on the point he felt was the proper site for the first boundary marker, but the two commissioners came to grips with their differences at length. All parties signed the agreement even though the surveyor had yet to arrive from Texas. When Surveyor Gray saw the Bartlett-García Conde agreement he disapproved, and heated words were exchanged. Surveyor Whipple also asserted in turn that the point was too far north. Now Bartlett's three major scientists were all set in opposition to him. Public sentiment and an outcry from congress could be heard 'way out west: the boundary line is

[22] Gray Sweeney, "Drawing Borders: Art and the Cultural Politics of the U.S.-Mexico Boundary Survey, 1850-1853," in Sweeney and Grassham, *Drawing the Borderline*, pp. 31-33.

[23] *Ibid.*

[24] Goetzmann, *Army Exploration*, p. 173.

[25] Bartlett, *Personal Narrative*, Vol. 1, p. 210.

too far north. But Bartlett held firm with the Mexican commissioner and so the initial point was actually set just west of Doña Ana, New Mexico. [26]

On April 24, 1851, a ceremony was held at that site. A small obelisk was erected to contain the documents of the event. Given the task that lay ahead, commissioners Bartlett and García Conde set out to follow conscientiously the guidelines which were outlined in the Treaty of Guadalupe Hidalgo. Their task would continue to be very difficult. Confusion over the boundary's initial point led to continuing controversy to which were added political pressures for a transcontinental railroad route through the disputed territory. Sectional differences also contributed to the upheaval over the boundary work. These problems and others preoccupied congress and the boundary commission over the next two years. [27]

The Bartlett-García Conde boundary line clearly diminished the size of the United States' war prize. Land now to continue under the Mexican flag included valuable terrain that the United States wanted. One of the reasons the United States went to war was to expand through Mexico's far northern frontier. The area held potential for a transcontinental railroad. Lieutenant Colonel James D. Graham, Topographical Engineers, newly arrived, believed he had final scientific authority over the survey and also opposed the location of the first marker. He proceeded to bar Bartlett from obtaining supplies, and refused to work further on the survey until Bartlett submitted to his claim of authority. Bartlett immediately fired letters off to Washington and, in time, Graham was removed. Once again Emory came back to serve on the commission, now with the rank of major. But it was too late. Hard feelings and heated accusations plagued Bartlett not only in the field but also in Washington. [28]

Expansionist Democrats cried foul and demanded explanations. Bartlett finally suspended the survey and asked his Mexican counterpart to do the same. García Conde refused, declaring that the delays were hurting the complicated, expensive process. He thus continued to work ahead while Bartlett tried to figure out what to do next. An all-out public outcry was developing in which a major participant was none other than the new U.S. senator from California, the second boundary commissioner, John Weller. Bartlett could hardly have had worse luck in his ever more tangled commission work. [29]

Everyone was able ultimately to finish the survey work, however. The American and Mexican teams worked their way to the Gila River and on to the Colorado, completing the boundary by linking to work done earlier from San Diego. While seeking needed supplies for his team in Santa Cruz and Magdalena, Mexico, Bartlett contracted typhoid fever. Ill and too frail to join the commission in day-to-day work, Bartlett sweated out his fever in the Mexican interior. He could not resist studying the Yaqui and other Native American groups from the surrounding areas while he recuperated, reflecting his long-standing ethnographic interests. [30]

---

[26] *Ibid.*, pp. 175-178; Faragher, "North, South," pp. 7-9; Hine, *Bartlett's West*, p. 32.
[27] Goetzmann, *Army Exploration*, pp. 175-178.
[28] Hine, *Bartlett's West*, p. 83.
[29] *Ibid.*, p. 82.
[30] Bartlett, *Personal Narrative*, Vol. 1, p. 443.

Once revitalized and en route to Guaymas, Bartlett learned that his friend and co-commissioner García Conde had died from typhus. Bartlett wrote in his journal on December 24, 1851, that word had arrived:

> ... bringing [the] painful news that General García Conde ... had died [in Arispe] on the 19th .... General García Conde was but 47 years of age. He was an accomplished engineer, and a most amiable and estimable gentleman. Our intercourse had been of the most friendly and agreeable character; and he had ever shown himself ready to aid the American Commission .... [H]e had filled many important positions under his government, among which I may mention those of Secretary of War and the Navy, Director of Military College, and Deputy from the State of Sonora to the Mexican Congress. [31]

From Guaymas Bartlett traveled to Mazatlan where he boarded a steamer to San Diego to rejoin the commission. The members who were there had only recently learned of Bartlett's brush with death. With health restored Bartlett decided that, while in California, it was important to visit San Francisco and the surrounding areas. [32]

Other commission members were still or again in El Paso, continuing to work on the boundary line. Transfers and new arrivals came and went from this border town, notably Major Emory as noted above. He wrote in a letter on January 15, 1852:

> On my arrival here I found things more complicated than I had expected, a large party, half with Colonel Graham at this place, and the other half with Mr. Bartlett God-knows-where, the whole numbering one hundred and upwards, no money, no credit, subdivided amongst themselves and the bitterest feeling between the different parties.

It did not take Emory very long to understand the problem, only to state the obvious. Making the most of the situation, Emory deliberately failed to sign the boundary documents giving Mexico the land west of the Río Grande up to Doña Ana. Emory carefully failed to sign the initial-point documents, thus leaving a loophole for his Democratic friends to make the most of at a later date. [33]

After leaving San Diego in May 1852, Bartlett and his part of the survey team headed east to the Gila country of present Arizona. Mid-day temperatures rose to 108°, so they would travel at night if there were enough light from the moon. Artist Pratt wrote in his diary on July 13 of some of the difficulties of night travel:

> About 11 oclk, no moon & the night very dark, we could only get glimpses of the road and other objects by the flash of lightening, which were frequent with heavy thunder, In the midst of this we suddenly found our party mixed up with a large party of emigrants on their way

---

[31] *Ibid.*, p. 457.
[32] *Ibid.*, Vol. 2, p. 3.
[33] Goetzmann, *Army Exploration*, p. 182; citation from draft letter to James A. Pearce.

from Texas to California, some of whom were in wagons, others on mules & horses ... . Our pack mules became mixed up with theirs, and caused some confusion and [detention] and in the obscurity one of ours was lost so that one of our people went ... back to ... recover it. [34]

Pratt and Bartlett both noted that there was a great concern over the danger that nomadic Indians would attack the surveyors. Pratt wrote that, as the survey party approached a group of Pima Indians after 11:00 at night, the normally peaceful Pimas feared that the commission members were Apaches:

> ... as we were coming direct from the Apache country the first glance at us, started them, as they are at war with the Apaches, and the day before had killed 4 of them and taken 3 prisoners. We soon came to cultivated fields ... [W]e could hear the Indians calling to each other in all directions, the Apache! The Apache!, no it is the Americans ... as soon as they found they had no chance for a fight they laughed heartily on all sides at the false alarm and panic ... . [35]

Weary but yet determined, the boundary commission party pressed on, completing all details of the survey from San Diego to Fort Yuma. Moving then up the Gila River, they surveyed very slowly, but the work did progress. Bartlett found the daily personal oversight of the project ever so tedious. Finally he could stand it no longer and moved to the Pima villages, whence he toured the area and gave special attention to the Casa Grande ruins. As was the case throughout the boundary survey, Bartlett often paid far more attention to non-survey activities than to the work for which he was being compensated. [36]

Not surprisingly, money ran short for the commission. Congress appropriated another $100,000 to see the project through to its completion. By 1852 the project was plagued by complaints about the amount of time Bartlett was taking and about the exorbitant costs. Many New York and Washington newspapers lambasted Bartlett for poor management of the commission. Usually there were added commentaries by former commission members and known Bartlett enemies such as Weller, Graham, Emory and others. Each accused Bartlett with, among other things, serious financial mismanagement.

For Bartlett the handwriting on the wall could be recognized clearly. As the new president was elected, Bartlett's adversaries moved in to halt his continuation as head of the commission. It was not very long before congress withdrew the appropriation for completion of the survey, and of course Bartlett's position was terminated. However, early in 1853, while reading a New Orleans newspaper, Bartlett learned that a new appropriation by congress had been provided, allowing the survey to proceed. Bartlett wrote:

---

[34] Pratt MS diary, July 13, 1852; unpublished, private owner.
[35] *Ibid.*, July 4, 1852.
[36] Bartlett, *Personal Narrative*, Vol. 2, pp. 285f.

But the commission had been broken up; the injury had already been inflicted upon its members, who were now scattered and on their way to their homes; and it was too late to return to the field of operations.

Bartlett telegraphed the secretary of the interior that there was no way the commission could now pick up and continue. [37]

In disregard of this advice, Bartlett was replaced by a southerner, Robert Blair Campbell, but the latter's tenure was short for the survey was definitively canceled later in the year. Political changes in Washington were the reality; expense was a ready excuse if any were needed. The boundary question was ultimately settled by purchase of the coveted land from Mexico, by the 1853 Gadsden Purchase Treaty or Treaty of Mesilla. The area involved encompassed the southernmost part of present Arizona and southwestern part of New Mexico.

Bartlett had to defend himself in Washington against a lengthy list of charges but it amounted to no more than placing him in embarrassing situations. The expenditures for the three-year, two thousand-mile survey had soared from the original estimate of $100,000 to $500,000.

Bartlett's greatest disappointment came when the government refused to publish his *Personal Narrative*. He had hoped to make a lasting mark through this book. Realizing that there was no hope of the government publishing it, as had been done for comparable projects of exploration, etc., Bartlett eventually self-published it. The two-volume *Personal Narrative of Explorations and Incidents in Texas, New Mexico, California, Sonora, and Chihuahua, 1850-1853* is a highly detailed account of the survey leadership, scientific explorations, and study of aboriginal peoples. Bartlett thought of himself as the extended arm of the great eastern scientific community, and also as an artist. His work stands as a sort of monument, not only to the high cost of the survey but also to greatly increased knowledge about the borderland regions Bartlett studied so avidly. As a footnote to his varied career, prior to his death in 1881 Bartlett served with distinction many years as Rhode Island's secretary of state and as librarian for the John Carter Brown Library of Brown University. [38]

[37] *Ibid.* (Jan. 11, 1853).
[38] Hine, *Bartlett's West*, pp. 91-93.

MARK J. STEGMAIER

Mark J. Stegmaier, professor of history and former chair of the department at Cameron State University, Lawton, Oklahoma, received his B.A. in history from the University of Santa Clara, M.A. and Ph.D. from the University of California, Santa Barbara. He is a specialist in American ante-bellum political history.

His first major book, *Texas, New Mexico, and the Compromise of 1850: Boundary Dispute and Sectional Crisis* (Kent, OH: Kent State University Press, 1996) won the Coral H. Tullis Prize of the Texas State Historical Society as the outstanding book on Texas history in 1996, and the Villagrá Award from the Historical Society of New Mexico in 1998. The winning of these awards from societies that do not always perceive all aspects of the past in the same way speaks volumes for the evenhandedness as well as high quality of Stegmaier's treatment. The work is a detailed analysis of a complex situation made more complex by the skillful maneuvering of some of the greatest legislators in American history. His writing skill, however, is such that he escorts the reader through a maze of arcane political and parliamentary maneuvers without losing the reader's interest.

Stegmaier's essay below is an expansion and extension of material included in his book. It is, however, more than simply a reworking of previously published material. If former House Speaker "Tip" O'Neill's aphorism is true, that "All politics is local," Professor Stegmaier surely suggests with reason that "All history is local."

Stegmaier demonstrates in a very convincing manner the importance of a minor event, the sale of some land at the village of Doña Ana, New Mexico, in shaping the national debate on something as important as the Compromise of 1850. The event was the sale of a headright (land claim) at Doña Ana by a representative of the State of Texas to a U.S. Army officer. This occurred after the U.S.-Mexican War but before U.S. territorial government was organized in New Mexico, while Texas attempted to make good on its boundary claim to the left bank of the whole length of the Río Grande.

The impact of this sale, a clear violation of the land-holding guarantees of the Treaty of Guadalupe Hidalgo, reverberated throughout New Mexico. In the course of time reports of it reached the floor of congress where references to it appeared in senate debates on the Texas-New Mexico boundary dispute. This dispute was, as Professor Stegmaier documents, a crucial element of the Compromise of 1850. In fact, Stegmaier concludes, the boundary bill may have been the crucial block in the elaborate and delicate edifice Henry Clay designed and Stephen A. Douglas brought to fruition. Stegmaier's logic is persuasive. As he demonstrates, Texas made repeated threats to send troops to enforce its boundary claim. The Taylor and Fillmore administrations countered these threats with statements indicating that they would order the U.S. Army to block Texas forces. Southern fire-brands insisted that troops from their other respective states would support Texas in such a conflict. Thus Stegmaier suggests that the Civil War might have started a decade sooner had this problem not been resolved in an equitable manner. Had that resolution not occurred, the history of the nation would have been significantly different.

That it did not happen does not minimize the impact of events in a small, dusty New Mexico town almost 150 years ago. The strength of Stegmaier's essay lies not only in its explication of importance of this seemingly minor event but also in demonstrating once again that both the *pluribus* and the *unum* are an integral part of our nation's past.

G.L. Seligmann
University of North Texas

THE GUADALUPE HIDALGO TREATY AS A FACTOR

IN THE NEW MEXICO-TEXAS BOUNDARY DISPUTE

Mark J. Stegmaier

Of the many issues bedeviling the nation in the late 1840s and gradually loosening the bonds of the union, building up to the Civil War of 1861-1865, one of the least noticed by past historians has been the boundary dispute between New Mexico and Texas. That controversy has proved to be much more significant in the sectional crisis and Compromise of 1850 than previous historians have recognized. Among the other divisive issues facing congress in 1850—California statehood, slavery and government organization for Utah and New Mexico, the Texas debt, the fugitive slave law, the slave trade in the District of Columbia—none proved so immediately threatening to the continuance of the union in 1850 nor so instrumental in resolving the other issues in the great compromise as the New Mexico-Texas boundary dispute.

This essay focuses only in part on summarizing the boundary controversy and its significance. Nineteen ninety-eight marks the 150th anniversary of the Treaty of Guadalupe Hidalgo, which ended the Mexican-American War. That treaty, certain provisions of it in particular, became relevant to the New Mexico-Texas boundary dispute, and these provisions entered into the dynamics of the boundary issue during the sectional crisis of 1848-1850. The treaty articles and the boundary dispute even became intermingled with the fate of the small village of Doña Ana, New Mexico.

The New Mexico-Texas boundary dispute originated in the 1680s French claim by explorer René Robert Cavelier, Sieur de La Salle, to all lands which drained into the Mississippi River and all lands east of the Río Grande.[1] This French claim to what they called Louisiana conflicted with Spanish claims and settlement in the region. New Mexico was founded in 1598 and the Spanish had established missions and outposts in Texas in the 1690s. When France sold the Louisiana Purchase to the United States in 1803, President Thomas Jefferson revived the notion that Louisiana included Texas and everything east of the Río Grande. The Río Grande thus entered American consciousness as the claimed southwestern boundary of Texas, the Louisiana Purchase, and the United States, regardless of provincial boundaries that Spain had established north of the river. In the 1819 Adams-Onís Treaty, the United States retreated from the Río Grande claim and established the line between U.S. and Spanish possessions at the Sabine River, Red River, 100° west longitude, and so forth.

---

[1] Rupert N. Richardson, *Texas: The Lone Star State* (New York: Prentice-Hall, Inc., 1943), pp. 22-23.

When Mexico became independent of Spain in 1821 and opened Texas to American settlement soon after, Americans arrived in Texas imbued with the conviction that the Río Grande was the southwestern boundary of Texas, even though the Mexican government's provincial boundary of Texas lay well north of the Río Grande, along the Medina and Nueces rivers. During the Texas Revolution of 1835-1836, Texas leaders constantly spoke of the Río Grande as their boundary with Mexico. After the decisive battle of San Jacinto, General Antonio López de Santa Anna was forced to agree to a treaty which strongly implied that the Río Grande was the boundary.[2] The Mexican government quickly renounced Santa Anna's treaty but on December 19, 1836, the Texas Congress passed a law unilaterally declaring that the boundary of the republic on the southwest extended from the mouth of the Río Grande upriver to its source and from that point northward to the 1819 U.S.-Spanish treaty line at 42° north latitude.[3] Texas thus laid its official claim to the settled area of the Mexican province of New Mexico. The United States extended diplomatic recognition to Texas in March 1837 at the end of President Andrew Jackson's administration. New Mexicans disdained the Texas claim, however, and repelled Texan efforts to extend jurisdiction over New Mexico in the 1840s.

After President John Tyler failed to annex Texas by a treaty in 1844, congress decided to do it in early 1845 by joint resolutions which Texas agreed to accept. These resolutions did not specify a boundary for Texas, presumably leaving that matter for negotiation between the United States and Mexico. Several clauses of the resolutions seemed to imply that the United States was annexing Texas with its boundaries as Texas claimed them.[4] Texas and the next American president, James K. Polk, certainly understood the resolutions that way. Mexico, however, still considered Texas to be one of her provinces, and refused to recognize Texas independence or any U.S. right to annex it. The Mexican government refused to deal with Polk on the matter.

These circumstances led inexorably to war by 1846. In one of the first military operations General Stephen Watts Kearny led an army including Missouri volunteers to Santa Fé and in August 1846 bloodlessly took possession of New Mexico. In an official proclamation and more specifically in a private message to Governor Manuel Armijo, Kearny cited as authority for his conquest the original 1836 Texas boundary law,[5] but subsequently he totally ignored the Texas claim to New Mexico. Kearny quickly established an occupation government with jurisdiction on both banks of the Río Grande.

Following the U.S. conquest of New Mexico, Texas reasserted its 1836 claim but the Polk administration ignored Texan entreaties and continued the civil government begun by Kearny. In March 1848 the U.S. Senate approved and President Polk ratified the Treaty of Guadalupe Hidalgo to end the war. The treaty did not particularly relate to the boundary between New Mexico and

---

[2] *Ibid.,* pp. 136-137; and Mark J. Stegmaier, *Texas, New Mexico, and the Compromise of 1850: Boundary Dispute and Sectional Crisis* (Kent, OH: Kent State University Press, 1996), pp. 6-7.

[3] *Laws of the Republic of Texas* (1838), pp. 133-134.

[4] William W. Freehling, *The Road to Disunion,* Vol. 1: *Secessionists at Bay, 1776-1854* (New York: Oxford University Press, 1990), pp. 440-449.

[5] Thomas S. Edrington, "Military Influence on the Texas-New Mexico Boundary Settlement," *New Mexico Historical Review,* Vol. 59 (Oct. 1984), pp. 374-375.

Texas, but some articles and the map attached to it provided material for arguments in congress on both sides of that issue.[6]

Also in March 1848 the Texas legislature created on paper a huge Santa Fé County comprised of the entire region between the Pecos River and the Río Grande, including the entire northwestern segment of the 1836 claim.[7] Texas designated this county as its 11th Judicial District but Texan judge Spruce M. Baird found his weak efforts to organize this county-district blocked by U.S. and New Mexican officials when he arrived at Santa Fé. In Washington the first session of the 30th Congress considered proposals to resolve the issue of civil governments in the Mexican Cession, but controversy over the status of slavery there ruined any chance for these plans to pass.

General Zachary Taylor, Mexican War hero, won the election of 1848 and succeeded Polk as president in March 1849. Although he was a Louisiana slaveholder, Taylor alienated himself from southerners, even his own southern Whigs, by adopting policies which seemed to favor northern free-soil interests in the Mexican Cession. The short second session of the 30th Congress in 1849 failed to settle the slavery issue or the concomitant civil government question. Taylor then launched his own initiative by dispatching emissaries to California and New Mexico to encourage the people there to bypass the territorial stage of political development and request immediate admission to the union as states. Taylor ignored the fact that, in the previous congressional session, a convention at Santa Fé had petitioned only for the territorial form of government, without slavery. Taylor wanted to pursue a simplistic solution to the territorial slavery issue, taking it for granted that no objection would be made if statehood constitutional conventions rather than territorial legislatures opposed slavery in California and New Mexico.

California acceded to Taylor's wishes and framed a state constitution, but U.S. Indian Agent James S. Calhoun, Taylor's man in New Mexico, found little enthusiasm for statehood there. Instead, New Mexico organized another convention in September 1849 which again petitioned for territorial government, and this time made no reference to slavery in its petition. Neither this nor the previous convention pressed for recognition of a specific boundary.

When Texans learned of the second New Mexico convention, their legislature and new governor, Peter H. Bell, reacted belligerently. They even threatened to send troops to Santa Fé to put down what one legislator called the "greasers" revolt. The legislature also divided the unwieldy Santa Fé County into four, with the largest and most northerly being the new Santa Fé County, which still was so large as to embrace the present Doña Ana County, New Mexico.[8] Governor Bell appointed a new commissioner, former U.S. Indian Agent Robert S. Neighbors, to organize governments in all four counties. Meanwhile President Taylor delegated a new agent, Colonel George A. McCall, to act more aggressively than Calhoun in pushing New Mexico to seek statehood. McCall

---

[6] For the treaty and related documents see Richard Griswold del Castillo, *The Treaty of Guadalupe Hidalgo: A Legacy of Conflict* (Norman: University of Oklahoma Press, 1990), pp. 179-199.

[7] Stegmaier, *Texas, New Mexico,* p. 27.

[8] *Laws of the Third Legislature of the State of Texas* (1850), pp. 24-25.

reached Santa Fé before the Texan commissioner, for Neighbors spent time organizing El Paso County in February and March 1850.

While Neighbors was at Doña Ana an incident occurred which severely compromised his mission and destroyed any possibility of the Texan receiving a favorable reception at Santa Fé. Doña Ana citizens of Mexican descent were frightened into believing that their property rights, guaranteed to them under Article IX of the recent Treaty of Guadalupe Hidalgo, were in jeopardy. Unbeknownst to Neighbors, one of his assistants named William Cockburn sold the U.S. Army post commander at Doña Ana, Major Enoch Steen, a Texas headright to a 640-acre parcel which included the village of Doña Ana. Even though Neighbors himself did not learn of this transaction until he returned from Santa Fé in May, local New Mexican landowners somehow heard about it and realized that this adverse claim threatened property titles which they believed were protected under the Treaty of Guadalupe Hidalgo. These citizens, including Guadalupe Miranda, Rafael Ruelas, Miguel Montoya and more than forty others, signed a protest (appended below) written in Spanish by Miranda and sent it directly to Col. John A. Munroe, military governor at Santa Fé.[9] They argued that Steen's headright violated their natural rights and the guarantees of security for property rights originally made by General Kearny and confirmed in the 1848 treaty.

Colonel Munroe chose to mention nothing about this matter to Neighbors during the latter's brief and fruitless effort in Santa Fé to thwart a Munroe-McCall-orchestrated statehood convention movement. Munroe instead wrote to his subordinate, Major Steen, demanding an explanation and lecturing him on the evil impact of his Texas headright on the citizens of Doña Ana. Munroe stated that this headright might panic many of the local populace into abandoning their property and moving elsewhere.

Later that year, in fact, Rafael Ruelas and others did establish the town of La Mesilla on the western bank of the Río Grande, outside of any possible Texan claim and, they believed, on the Mexican side of the international boundary which was yet to be surveyed. (The Bartlett-Conde line did leave Mesilla on the Mexican side, but then the Gadsden Purchase of 1853 placed Mesilla in U.S. jurisdiction.) The U.S. Army dealt quietly with Steen, removing him temporarily from New Mexico and sending him east to defend his actions to the adjutant general. Another officer was court-martialed for offenses which included feeding Neighbors's animals from army supplies, and also sent east. The treaty rights of the Doña Ana population were honored, Steen's Texas headright was not.

While all this was transpiring in New Mexico the 31st Congress was searching in 1850 for a peaceful solution to the boundary dispute and other issues in a crisis that many believed would end that year in disunion and civil war between northern and southern states. The New Mexico-Texas boundary dispute gradually supplanted all other issues in the public mind as the single most volatile issue. The reason was that the boundary issue alone, with its threat of Texas troops invading New

---

[9] The petition is located in documents transmitted to Washington from the 9th Military Department. Bvt. Col. John A. Munroe to Adj. Gen. Roger Jones, May 20, 1850, in M-567 (Letters Received by the Office of the Adjutant General, Main Series, 1822-1860), roll 432, item M-312; Record Group 94 (Records of the Adjutant General's Office), National Archives.

Mexico and engaging U.S. military forces there, might provide the spark sufficient to ignite a general conflict.[10]

Many proposals for resolving the boundary question and even for subdividing Texas were offered early in the 31st Congress, including an "Omnibus Bill" embracing all territorial issues, which proposed a New Mexico-Texas line running from a point twenty miles north of El Paso northeastward to the intersection of 100° west longitude and the Red River. Debate was incessant, vigorous and rancorous on the Omnibus Bill in the senate. President Taylor became ill in July and died, succeeded by Millard Fillmore of New York, who was more inclined to compromise. The Omnibus Bill itself was dismantled in the senate on July 31 over the boundary issue.

A series of separate bills was then constructed to encompass all parts of the defunct bill. The boundary bill included provisions for the present-day New Mexico-Texas line. This bill, involving the fate of the union more than any of the other measures, and being the prerequisite for passage of the others, became the first in the set passed in the senate in August. President Fillmore contributed an important special message in the crisis, warning Texas that he would invoke his powers as commander-in-chief to repel any Texan invasion of New Mexico. His secretary of state, Daniel Webster, reiterated this warning in a letter to Governor Bell of Texas. The U.S. House of Representatives took up the senate bills and, after much debate and parliamentary procedure, passed a bill combining the boundary, payment of the Texas debt, and establishment of New Mexico Territory on September 6. The senate concurred in this "Little Omnibus," the other bills passed the house, Fillmore signed them all, colorful celebrations in Washington and other cities hailed the compromise, and the Texas Legislature accepted the compromise in November.[11]

During the months of debate which produced this Compromise of 1850, many speeches in congress concerned the New Mexico-Texas boundary dispute. Supporters on both sides of the controversy invoked the authority of the Treaty of Guadalupe Hidalgo on behalf of their viewpoints. These arguments built upon a foundation laid down in congress in two 1848 speeches concerning the boundary dispute, after President Polk communicated the exchange of treaty ratifications by the United States and Mexico to congress.

On July 27, 1848, Representative David Kaufman, a Texas Democrat, had ardently defended the position held by Texas and southern Democrats, that the entire region of New Mexico east of the Río Grande legitimately belonged to Texas. Kaufman argued that the Texas annexation resolutions of 1845 in numerous ways had recognized and reinforced the Texas boundary claim. Kaufman asserted that the U.S. government, according to the annexation resolutions, had agreed to settle boundary issues with Mexico and acted as Texas's agent in resorting to war over the Río Grande boundary and in securing Mexican acceptance of that boundary in the Treaty of Guadalupe Hidalgo. The congressman held that the treaty provisions in no way diminished the Texas claim to the whole region east of the Río Grande. He interpreted three particular sections of the annexation resolutions as implying U.S. recognition of the 1836 Texas claim: 1) Texas's right to subdivide into four additional states;

[10] Stegmaier, *Texas, New Mexico,* pp. 63-114.
[11] *Ibid.,* pp. 115-314.

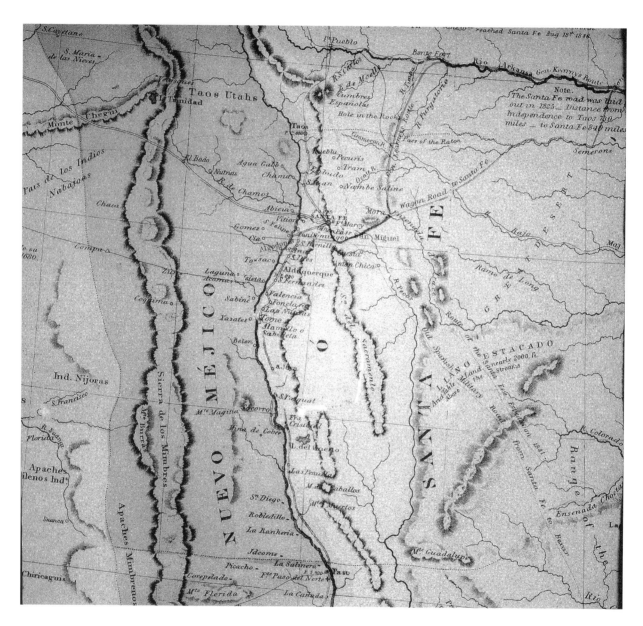

Central portion of Disturnell Map (1847). Note the vertical lettering, straddling the Río Grande: "NUEVO MEJICO/O/SANTA FE."

Courtesy: Center for American History, University of Texas, Austin.

2) prohibition of slavery in any states formed from Texas north of 36°30' (the Missouri Compromise line of 1820); and 3) Texas's pledge to use its public domain to pay off its debt. These provisions, Kaufman pointed out, made no sense unless the full extent of the Texas claim east of the Río Grande was valid.[12]

Representative Charles Hudson, a Massachusetts Whig, challenged Kaufman on August 8, 1848. Hudson expounded the view that, despite the Texas "paper" claim of 1836 and the implications of the Texas annexation resolutions, New Mexico east of the Río Grande had always been separate from Texas and had been ceded to the United States in the Guadalupe Hidalgo treaty by Mexico, which had held New Mexico as one of its provinces. Hudson pointed out that the United States had treated the Santa Fé region as separate from Texas prior to the war by maintaining a consul there. He spoke of the law passed just after the Texas annexation resolutions which allowed a drawback on U.S. customs duties on foreign goods transported across the United States to Santa Fé in their original packaging. He also cited the annexation resolutions themselves, specifically a section referring to the lands "properly included within, and rightfully belonging to" Texas. To Hudson and those who shared his views, this clause eliminated New Mexico east of the Río Grande from Texas's limits because Texas had never exercised actual possession of the region according to the international law principle of *uti possidetis* (*i.e.*, as you now possess).

In reference to the Treaty of Guadalupe Hidalgo, Hudson argued that the 1847 Disturnell map attached to the treaty was irrelevant to the New Mexico-Texas boundary question, despite Disturnell's use of different colors on either side of the Río Grande, because Disturnell had admitted that he colored the map thus with an eye to making it as marketable in Texas as possible. Hudson stated also that the treaty cited the map as authority only on the southern and western boundaries of New Mexico, not on the boundary between New Mexico and Texas. This Massachusetts Whig also expressed concern and that of other northerners over possible extension of slavery to New Mexico via the claim of slaveholding Texas. Hudson identified the Texas claim as the only realistic chance for slavery to spread to New Mexico, a point made forcefully and often in *New York Tribune* editorials by Horace Greeley, an inveterate champion of New Mexico's quest for governance separate from that of Texas.[13]

The New Mexico-Texas boundary dispute did not become a major point of debate in the struggle to provide territorial governments during the second session of the 30th Congress in early 1849. Greeley, serving briefly as a Whig congressman from New York during that session, did what he could to promote the establishment of civil government in New Mexico, as did Representative Caleb Smith, an Indiana Whig leader. But arguments based on the Treaty of Guadalupe Hidalgo were largely unheard in that session.[14]

It was in the titanic, nine-month, first session of the 31st Congress (December 1849-September 1840) that the New Mexico-Texas boundary dispute emerged as the issue which more than any

---

[12] *Congressional Globe,* 30th Cong., 1st sess., Appendix, pp. 785-786.
[13] *Ibid.,* pp. 927-928. For Greeley's attitude before 1850 see *New York Daily Tribune,* Mar. 19, Apr. 1, 24, 1847, and Jan. 17, Oct. 17, 15, 26, Nov. 1, 5, 6, 12, 20, 1849.
[14] Stegmaier, *Texas, New Mexico,* pp. 41-42.

other would settle the fate of the union. Although the slavery expansion issue did not enter directly into discourse on the boundary question very often in 1850, awareness of the dispute's relevance to the overall subject of slavery extension was always there, lurking just beneath the surface.[15]

Much debate over the New Mexico-Texas boundary in 1850, as it related to the Treaty of Guadalupe Hidalgo, focused on Articles V and IX. Article V defined the U.S.-Mexican boundary and parts of the New Mexico boundary, and cited an 1847 edition of Disturnell's "Mapa de los Estados Unidos de Mejico" as authoritative on the boundary. Article IX concerned the protection of rights of Mexican citizens in ceded lands until the incorporation of these areas into the union.

Texans and their supporters from other southern states emphasized Article V and the treaty map as corroborative of the 1836 Texas claim to New Mexico east of the Río Grande. Article V stated that the U.S.-Mexican boundary would begin at the mouth of the Río Grande, extend up that river to the "southern line of New Mexico," undesignated as to latitude, before proceeding westward. Article V also stated that the southern and western limits of New Mexico were those marked on the attached Disturnell map.[16] Although the treaty stated that the "southern line" was the one drawn on Disturnell's map, no one in congress in 1850 seemed to take that line very seriously. The actual location of the "southern line of New Mexico" was treated as a boundary yet to be determined.

The pro-Texas bloc argued that the Treaty of Guadalupe Hidalgo was irrelevant regarding territory east of the Río Grande since the Texas annexation resolutions and later documentary evidence had, in their opinion, confirmed boundaries claimed by Texas in 1836. On the other hand, they also argued that the Disturnell map showed all of New Mexico west of the Río Grande colored green while it depicted everything east of the Río Grande in white as part of Texas.

Texans, particularly Thomas Jefferson Rusk in the senate and Volney Howard in the house of representatives, reiterated and elaborated upon the arguments voiced in 1848 by Representative Kaufman that the annexation resolutions of 1845 had implied acceptance of the 1836 Texas-claimed boundaries. Although the Polk and Taylor administrations had been inconsistent on this subject, the Texans cited various policy statements by Polk and his secretary of state, James Buchanan, and by Taylor and his secretary of war, George Crawford, to support their assertion. Only recently, the Texans said, had President Taylor and his administration transformed the temporary wartime civil-military government established by General Kearny in New Mexico into an adverse U.S. claim against Texas. The Texans argued that the U.S. government had acted as an agent or trustee of Texas in its military conquest of the Santa Fé region. They cited Kearny's proclamation at Las Vegas in August 1846 to support their conclusion. If only the Texans had known about the personal message by Kearny to Armijo, more specifically basing the U.S. possession on the 1836 Texas claim—a document discovered in the Mexican archives some years ago by Thomas Edrington—they could have strengthened this part of their argument enormously.[17]

---

[15] *Cong. Globe,* 31 Cong., 1 sess., App., pp. 679-681, 1083. These speeches relating the boundary conflict to slavery extension were by Sen. Thomas Hart Benton (D-MO), a fervent and consistent defender of New Mexico, and Rep. Alexander H. Stephens (W-GA), an ardent defender of the Texas claim.

[16] Griswold del Castillo, *Treaty,* p. 187.

[17] *Cong. Globe,* 31 Cong., 1 sess., pp. 207-209; App. pp. 236, 870-871, 976, 1421-1422; and n. 5 above.

Given their argument that U.S. occupation of New Mexico east of the Río Grande was in fulfillment of the Texas annexation resolutions, it was only logical for Texans to declare that Article V of the Guadalupe Hidalgo treaty accorded with their claim. The article itself included nothing specifically about the area east of the Río Grande, but referred only to the southern and western limits of New Mexico. And the Disturnell map appeared, by its coloring, to place all of New Mexico west of the Río Grande. The Texans questioned why any distinction was now being made by the federal government between the upper and lower Río Grande. The United States had posited no adverse claim to Texas jurisdiction in the area along the northern bank of the lower Río Grande, even though Texas had exercised no actual jurisdiction over that region before the U.S.-Mexican War.[18] The Texans, and more especially Whig Representative Alexander Stephens of Georgia, portrayed the whole adverse U.S. claim to New Mexico east of the Río Grande as disingenuous, a concoction of antislavery northern politicians seeking to divest Texas and the slave states of their legitimate territory so that a free state could be erected therein.[19]

Northern antislavery elements in congress, along with some moderate southerners, did favor a New Mexico independent of Texas, lying on both sides of the Río Grande. Historically, they pointed out, New Mexico had never been under Texas jurisdiction. To champions of New Mexico, the Texas annexation resolutions of 1845, no matter what the vague implications of some sections might have been, did not clearly establish a U.S. recognition of the Texas boundary claim. In fact, as Whig Senator Roger S. Baldwin of Connecticut showed, the U.S. government continued to treat New Mexico as Mexican territory even after adoption of the resolutions, by its drawback law and by its continued maintenance of a consul at Santa Fé. In 1845 President Polk's secretary of state, Buchanan, included in his instructions to John Slidell, U.S. emissary to Mexico, a directive to purchase New Mexico along with other territory from Mexico. Why would Polk, the pro-New Mexico bloc asked, attempt to purchase what was already U.S. territory as claimed by Texas? New Mexico's advocates also twisted the 1846 Kearny proclamation to serve their viewpoint. True, Kearny did claim New Mexico for the United States by virtue of the annexation resolutions, but his proclamation also claimed New Mexico on both sides of the Río Grande, and Kearny oversaw the establishment of civil government with jurisdiction on both sides of the river. Friends of New Mexico cited support given by Polk and Taylor to the Kearny government as evidence that their administrations did not consider the Texas claim valid.[20]

Senators Robert Baldwin (W-CT), Thomas Hart Benton (D-MO), and Joseph Underwood (W-KY), and Representative Andrew Ewing (W-TN) in 1850 were the primary defenders in congress of New Mexico's claim to separate identity from Texas. To them, New Mexico had been a province of Mexico until the war, with nearly all its settled communities on the eastern side of the Río Grande. Texas, they said, despite its 1836 claim, had constitutionally and legislatively ignored the Santa Fé region—until its belated, recent efforts to organize Texas counties along the upper Río

---

[18] *Ibid.,* pp. 207, 209; App. pp. 236, 871, 976, 1421-1422, 1431, 1478.
[19] *Ibid.,* App. p. 1083.
[20] *Ibid.,* App. pp. 814, 1028, 1110-1111, 1155-1157, 1169, 1171, 1184, 1197-1200, 1430.

Grande. During the whole pre-war period and even after U.S. occupation, New Mexico had functioned as an organized political community independent of Texas on both sides of the river. New Mexico's supporters claimed that the United States, not Texas, had captured New Mexico; that New Mexico had then become a U.S. possession; and that the Treaty of Guadalupe Hidalgo officially transferred New Mexico as an organized community from Mexican to U.S. jurisdiction, not that of Texas.[21]

Senator Underwood in particular resurrected the argument made by Representative Hudson of Massachusetts in 1848, that the upper Río Grande region was not "rightfully" included within Texas at annexation because Texas had never subjected the Santa Fé region to actual Texas possession and jurisdiction, *i.e.,* the principle of *uti possidetis*.[22] Senators Thomas J. Rusk and Sam Houston and representatives Volney Howard (D-TX), Humphrey Marshall (W-KY), and Henry Hilliard (W-AL) countered that New Mexico, following the conquest and the Guadalupe Hidalgo treaty, had been obliterated as a political community and that the term "New Mexico" now applied only to undefined geography. Texans and their like-minded colleagues held that Mexico had transferred geography and individual persons, not a political community with legal jurisdiction east of the Río Grande; to Texans this meant that they could still claim everything east of the river as being within the state's limits, no matter what separate existence New Mexico might once have had.[23]

The champions of New Mexico interpreted Article V of the treaty and the Disturnell map very differently. The most aggressively pro-New Mexico analyst of the treaty was Senator Underwood, who had opposed the U.S.-Mexican War as unjust and believed that the Nueces River was the proper southern boundary of Texas. He argued vehemently that close scrutiny of the wording of Article V and the Disturnell map conclusively decided the issue against Texas. According to Article V, the Río Grande boundary between the United States and Mexico intersected a point on the southern boundary of New Mexico. Underwood declared that reference to a "point" on that line implied that the treaty commissioners believed that the southern line also stretched east from that point on the Río Grande, meaning that New Mexico lay on both sides of the river. Underwood pointed out that the Disturnell map, despite use of different colors on either side of the river, actually showed the dotted, colored line designating the southern boundary of New Mexico to continue eastward from the Río Grande and then to turn north until it intersected the Red River. Also, as Underwood discerned, Disturnell's map had the words *Nuevo Mejico* printed on the western side of the Río Grande and *O' Santa Fé* printed on the eastern side, indicating that "New Mexico or Santa Fé" (in English translation) lay on both sides of the Río Grande, not merely on the western side as Texans and radical southern Democrat Representative James Seddon of Virginia and others claimed repeatedly and vociferously.[24]

---

[21] *Ibid.,* App. pp. 680, 813-814, 1028, 1110-1111, 1155-1157, 1169, 1171, 1195, 1197-1198, 1430.

[22] *Ibid.,* App. pp. 679, 681, 813, 1155, 1171, 1196-1197.

[23] *Ibid.,* App. pp. 977, 1151, 1191, 1430-1431, 1478.

[24] For Underwood's views see *ibid.,* App. pp. 1197-1200; for those of Seddon and the Texans see *ibid.,* p. 209; App. pp. 236, 871, 976, 1115, 1421, 1431, 1478.

When it came to debating the relevance of Article IX of the Guadalupe Hidalgo treaty to the New Mexico-Texas boundary dispute, the pro-New Mexico bloc most eagerly cited this article and forced Texans and their supporters on the defensive. Article IX fulfilled pledges originally made by General Kearny to the population of the conquered territories during the war for protection of civil liberties and property. The first part of the article promised that former Mexican citizens in these areas would be "incorporated in the Union" and "admitted, at the proper time," as adjudged by the U.S. Congress, to all the rights of U.S. citizens. The second part of Article IX promised that in the meantime the liberty, property and religion of former Mexican citizens would be "maintained and protected." When Hugh N. Smith applied unsuccessfully for admission to the U.S. House of Representatives as "delegate" from New Mexico, Ohio Whig John Taylor specifically favored his admission as a fulfillment of Article IX pledges on political rights. Volney Howard of Texas of course denounced Smith's application in a lengthy defense of the Texas position and denied that New Mexico still existed east of the Río Grande.[25]

To friends of New Mexico, Article IX clearly imposed the duty of protecting the rights of New Mexico's inhabitants on U.S. government officials until congress should decide to admit New Mexico as a state. Pro-New Mexico speakers in both senate and house reiterated this interpretation of the article, as did President Fillmore in his notable August 6, 1850, special message to congress, and also Secretary of State Daniel Webster in a letter of August 5 to Governor Bell of Texas. Article IX made sense to advocates of this position only if New Mexico lay on both sides of the Río Grande for, as Senator Benton particularly emphasized, virtually all the affected population in New Mexico was located on the eastern side of the river. Proponents of this view argued that Mexican commissioners had ceded New Mexico as a province lying on both sides of the river, as they understood it, and these commissioners intended the U.S. government to protect civil liberties on both sides of the river.[26]

The most radical proposal in favor of New Mexico was one to grant immediate statehood, a proposal devised and offered by northern Whig extremist Senator William H. Seward of New York. On July 26 the anti-compromise New Yorker suddenly proposed, at the height of tension over the Omnibus Bill, that New Mexico be admitted immediately as a free state under its recently adopted constitution. No official copy of this constitution had yet even arrived in Washington at that point! Earlier in the session President Taylor had favored statehood for both California and New Mexico, and on January 21 in a message to the senate had defended his sending emissaries to those two areas as a "faithful execution" of the treaty pledges in Article IX. But Seward's July 26 proposal, while a logical extension of Taylor's original plan, appeared to be a hopelessly extreme and needlessly provocative measure at this juncture.[27]

Senator Seward spoke in favor of his statehood amendment to the Omnibus Bill on July 26 in an address which embarrassed his unconsulted northern allies and shocked and angered moderates

---

[25] *Ibid.,* p. 1402; App. p. 976; and Griswold del Castillo, *Treaty,* p. 190.

[26] *Cong. Globe,* 31 Cong., 1 sess., App. pp. 1028, 1107, 1110-1111, 1122, 1156, 1169, 1171, 1195, 1430, 1439, 1442-1443, 1477-1478, 1565; James D. Richardson, comp., *A Compilation of the Messages and Papers of the Presidents, 1789-1897* (10 vols. Washington, DC: GPO, 1897), Vol. 5, p. 71; and Webster to Bell, Aug. 5, 1850, *House Executive Documents,* 31 Cong., 1 sess., 82 (serial 579), pp. 10-11.

[27] Stegmaier, *Texas, New Mexico,* pp. 95-97, 184-186.

and southern radicals. This speech is not as famous as his "Higher Law" speech earlier in the session but its sentiments, and notably the statehood proposal, elicited in retaliation from Senator Henry Foote of Mississippi the worst single example of verbal character assassination the senate experienced during the entire session. Seward argued that immediate statehood for New Mexico constituted the only effective way to fulfill the pledges to provide government and to protect people's rights guaranteed in the letter and spirit of Article IX of the Guadalupe Hidalgo treaty. Article IX guaranteed admission of New Mexico as a state "at the proper time," Seward insisted, and the time was now because New Mexico's liberties were threatened with subversion by a forced merger with Texas, and New Mexico's very political existence was threatened by Texan militia. Seward claimed that New Mexico possessed the requisite population for a state, more than 100,000 people, even if ninety percent of them were Indians and mixed bloods. Even Seward's friends would not entertain his statehood plan for New Mexico before an official copy of New Mexico's proposed constitution arrived in Washington. The amendment was defeated 42-1 at the end of the day, with Seward voting alone in its favor.[28]

The main implications of speeches by New Mexico's champions were not only that the U.S. government had a duty to enforce the guarantees of Article IX but also that Texas represented a clear threat that those pledges would be violated if New Mexico east of the Río Grande were included within the bounds of Texas. In essence this meant that the federal government had to protect New Mexico inhabitants east of the river or else rapacious Texans would pillage and plunder them. Fear of such an occurrence was not without foundation, given Major Steen's Texas headright at Doña Ana. Members of congress knew something about this headright, for Ohio Whig Senator Thomas Ewing made specific reference to it on August 8, 1850. More than likely, since information about the headright was confined to military correspondence from New Mexico, Ewing had been provided with this information by Winfield Scott, the army general-in-chief and acting secretary of war.

In his speech Ewing related how a U.S. military officer's Texas headright claim over Doña Ana had frightened local civilians into complaining to Colonel Munroe at Santa Fé. Ewing declared that the headright could influence people in the area, who dreaded Texans, to abandon their property and desert the region, a process which Ewing characterized as "forfeiture and confiscation." Since Ewing did not state how Steen had come by his headright, Senator Rusk of Texas seized upon this and got Ewing to admit that the headright claim, as far as he knew, involved only the U.S. commander at Doña Ana and not a Texan.[29]

While no one else in congress referred specifically to Steen's headright, the potential threat of Texas to New Mexicans' personal and property rights became a major theme of Representative Andrew Ewing, a moderate Tennessee Whig, on August 16. He held that New Mexico east of the Río Grande had been understood by the treaty commissioners as part of the ceded Mexican territory, not as part of Texas. Otherwise, Ewing pointed out, the reference to eventual incorporation into the

---

[28] *Cong. Globe,* 31 Cong., 1 sess., App. pp. 1442-1443.
[29] *Ibid.,* p. 1565.

union in Article IX would be absurd. And how could the United States pledge to protect citizens' rights in that area if it was already part of Texas? New Mexicans, Ewing declared, could control their own destiny and protect themselves from Texas only by becoming a separate U.S. territory and then state, for only in that process could the U.S. government protect rights promised under Article IX. If most of New Mexico, Ewing said, were forced to submit to Texan jurisdiction, then Texas could potentially pass laws denying the vote or other rights to Mexican-descended people of New Mexico, or requiring a religious test for voting or office-holding—laws which would negate the guarantees of Article IX and show bad faith by the United States in carrying out the treaty provisions. Representative Ewing favored the compromise plan to buy out the Texas claim, a valid claim he believed but one which conflicted with the international treaty obligations of the United States. A variation on Ewing's concerns had been sounded previously in the senate by Truman Smith, a Connecticut Whig, on July 8. Smith had argued that Article IX pledges on rights were inconsistent with the Texas claim for, if the Texas title east of the Río Grande were recognized as valid, then Texas might claim that its title had been valid since the 1836 Texas boundary law and set aside all land grants made under Mexican authority and vacate all property transfers made under Mexican law in New Mexico subsequent to that 1836 law.[30]

For advocates of the Texas claim, placed on the defensive by friends of New Mexico, the natural response was to argue that rights and liberties guaranteed under Article IX would be perfectly safeguarded under Texas jurisdiction east of the Río Grande, and therefore the Texas claim did not contravene the pledges of the Treaty of Guadalupe Hidalgo. This theme was particularly developed in speeches by Senator Houston on July 31 and representatives Seddon on August 13 and Hilliard on August 28. For these speakers the term "incorporated" in Article IX referred only to individual citizens, not to an organized political community called New Mexico. Democratic Senator Rusk and representatives Howard (Texas) and Marshall (Kentucky) agreed. It logically followed that citizens of Mexican descent residing east of the Río Grande could be "incorporated" into Texas and receive protection for their rights and liberties as citizens of that state, while the populace on the western side of the river could have their rights protected by federal government officials until they were "incorporated" into the union at the "proper time." The friends of Texas denied that New Mexico was intended under the treaty to be "incorporated" into the union as an existing political entity according to its earlier boundaries on both sides of the river; such an interpretation of Article IX misconstrued its meaning, they said.[31]

The most elaborate version of this argument was made by Representative Seddon, noted as an extremist. Seddon believed that any intimation that Texas would refuse to enforce Article IX provisions east of the Río Grande constituted a gratuitous insult to Texas. He pointed out that Texas had undertaken to exercise jurisdiction and presumably to protect Article IX rights in lower Río Grande areas where no actual Texan jurisdiction had existed before the war. Why should the upper

---

[30] *Ibid.,* pp. 1110-1111, 1184.
[31] *Ibid.,* pp. 977, 1115, 1151, 1191, 1430-1431, 1478, 1565.

Río Grande valley, also claimed by Texas on the left bank of the river since 1836, be treated any differently and subjected to an adverse claim by the U.S. government? Seddon also labeled it a "mockery" to hold that Texas jurisdiction in New Mexico east of the river was inconsistent with the Guadalupe Hidalgo treaty and simultaneously to require, as the compromise plans did, the assent of Texas to any settlement which congress passed?[32]

The question of the president's responsibilities in enforcing the Treaty of Guadalupe Hidalgo, particularly Article IX, emerged as a significant aspect of congressional debate over the boundary issue, especially after the threat of a Texan invasion of New Mexico and probable bloodshed between the invaders and U.S. military forces became more palpable scenarios. Congressional discussion of presidential powers became vigorous after Fillmore's message on August 6 revealed the administration's determination to use military force, if necessary, to protect New Mexico from a forcible takeover by Texas. Fillmore declared (words drafted mainly by Webster) that a treaty such as that of Guadalupe Hidalgo was a "supreme law of the land," that he had a solemn duty to enforce the provisions of that treaty, and that he possessed authority as commander-in-chief to employ U.S. armed forces and state militias in enforcing the treaty against hostile "combinations too powerful" to be resisted by the usual civil and judicial processes. Fillmore's message cited legal precedents for the executive's authority to use force in the militia acts of February 28, 1795, and March 3, 1807.[33]

While the U.S. Constitution in Article VI clearly included treaties as "supreme law of the land," some southerners such as Whig representatives Robert Toombs and Stephens of Georgia and Humphrey Marshall of Kentucky argued that the president's authority to enforce "supreme law" was not defined. Toombs and Stephens claimed that treaty Article IX did not specify that the president could employ military force to implement this section on his own authority. They held that the president could not use force legally without authorization by congress unless responding to explicit state resistance to a U.S. Supreme Court decision. Representative Robert McLane, Democrat of Maryland, strongly supported the views of the Georgia Whigs and accused Fillmore of "executive usurpation" of congressional powers in pledging to enforce Article IX by the bayonet if necessary. Representative Seddon of Virginia adopted the most extreme position uttered in the house on this issue, announcing his belief that the U.S. government possessed no constitutional authority to use force against a state's military force in order to enforce treaties or acts of congress.[34]

The response to the southern position on presidential powers came primarily from moderate northern Whig representatives George Ashmun of Massachusetts and William Duer of New York, and from northern antislavery Whig Representative Thaddeus Stevens of Pennsylvania. In speeches on August 14 and 15 these three vehemently defended the president's authority to fulfill the Guadalupe Hidalgo treaty's guarantees by force, without requiring any act of congress. They saw nothing in the

---

[32] *Ibid.,* p. 1115.

[33] Richardson, comp., *Messages,* Vol. 5, pp. 68-72. In April 1861, after the Confederate attack on Ft. Sumter, Pres. Lincoln would employ the authority of the 1795 militia act in calling out the initial 75,000 troops to put down the revellion. *Messages,* Vol. 6, p. 13; Richard N. Current, *Lincoln and the First Shot* (Philadelphia: J.B. Lippincott Co., 1963), p. 157.

[34] *Cong. Globe,* 31 Cong., 1 sess., App. pp. 1081, 1107, 1115, 1117-1118, 1122, 1150.

constitution requiring such an act before a president could enforce an international treaty. In certain cases such as a clause requiring an appropriation of funds, they admitted that congress might have a role in fulfilling treaty provisions. But Article IX was not such a case and Fillmore's supporters labeled it an absurdity to require a president to seek an act of congress before carrying out the executive responsibility to enforce treaties as "supreme law of the land."[35]

Duer of New York particularly attacked Seddon's extreme states' rights view as rendering all treaty obligations and acts of congress invalid. The president's constitutional authority to enforce laws and treaties was clear, he asserted, and no constitutional authority for state resistance existed. The duty to execute laws and treaties implied the exercise of military force when required, declared Duer. The pledges made to the people of New Mexico under Article IX operated *per se* and required no congressional law to reenact them. The rights and responsibilities of the president to defend New Mexico from Texan invasion were well established, Duer said. Texas possessed only a claim but no perfected title to the area east of the Río Grande.[36]

Representative Stevens of Pennsylvania delivered the strongest exposition in support of presidential military powers under the militia act of 1795. That act only stipulated, Stevens pointed out, that there exist hostile "combinations too powerful" for ordinary civil authorities to deal with before a president could exercise his powers to thwart them. Neither actual invasion nor actual state resistance to a judicial process need take place before the president could act. The mere threat of action by "combinations too powerful" would suffice to trigger a military response by the president, in this case to guarantee protection of treaty rights against a threatened Texan invasion.[37]

Southerners argued naturally that the president, if he did employ military force, should employ it to secure submission to Texan jurisdiction in the Santa Fé region. Democratic representatives John Savage and Andrew Johnson of Tennessee both made this argument. Johnson assumed a unique position in the debate, claiming that the Texas annexation resolutions of 1845 had been "in the nature of a treaty" with the Republic of Texas, were thus also to be enforced as "supreme law," and took precedence over the Treaty of Guadalupe Hidalgo.[38]

A major concern for the pro-Texas bloc in congress was that presidential use of military force in New Mexico would virtually settle the New Mexico-Texas boundary dispute in favor of New Mexico. Both President Fillmore in his August 6 message and Secretary of State Webster in his August 5 letter to the Texas governor declared that the administration's actions were not prejudicial to the Texas claim. Fillmore defended the U.S. Army presence in New Mexico as intended to protect the people of the disputed area from seizure or violence, as guaranteed under Article IX. But both insisted that the responsibility for defining the New Mexico-Texas boundary and establishing civil government for New Mexico rested squarely with congress. Until congress acted in these matters, the administration's duty according to Fillmore and Webster was to maintain the only actual jurisdiction since the U.S.-Mexican War in New Mexico—that set up by the government under Kearny in

---

[35] *Ibid.*, pp. 1107, 1122-1123, 1169, 1171.
[36] *Ibid.*, pp. 1169, 1171.
[37] *Ibid.*, p. 1107.
[38] *Ibid.*, pp. 1033, 1051.

1846. Entangled with these issues was the question of how the Fillmore administration would handle the proposed state constitution for New Mexico, drafted at Santa Fé under guidance from the previous administration.[39]

Southern concern over this matter was most particularly emphasized by Representative Robert McLane, Democrat of Maryland, in his critique of Fillmore's message. McLane also argued that the president would endorse New Mexico statehood once an official copy of its proposed constitution arrived in Washington. If Fillmore and his advisors had chosen to, as President Taylor almost certainly would have, they could have interpreted New Mexico's statehood movement and recently adopted constitution as a fulfillment of the guarantees of Article IX. Southerners dreaded that possibility, for it would mean another free state added to the union along with the anticipated admission of California. Southerners such as Representative Savage of Tennessee held that the actions of Colonels Munroe and McCall in organizing the New Mexico convention constituted a violation of Texan rights.[40]

Fillmore and Webster now had realized how sensitive southerners were about the Taylor administration's interference in New Mexico and sponsorship of New Mexico statehood. They therefore attempted to distance themselves from that movement without repudiating Munroe and McCall. Webster addressed this issue directly in writing Texas Governor Bell. He argued that Taylor's official instructions to McCall, through Secretary of War Crawford on November 19, 1849, had not defined the New Mexico-Texas boundary and therefore had not invaded the rights of Texas. Webster also informed Bell that the New Mexico constitutional convention, organized pursuant to McCall's orders, was a legitimate exercise of the right of a popular assembly to petition congress, but that the convention's authority extended no further than that. Webster wrote that the president would not approve of the recent New Mexico constitution if he considered its provisions hostile to the rights of either the United States or Texas. According to Webster, the president would deem this constitution a "nullity" until a proper tribunal had settled the boundary and established a government for New Mexico, and the president would treat the proposed constitution as a petition for statehood only, affecting the rights of neither party in the dispute until congress should take action.[41]

Southerners favoring the Texas claim interpreted the Fillmore-Webster documents and doctrines as evasive verbiage. As southerners saw it, the facts were that U.S. military forces did occupy New Mexico and exercised jurisdiction in place of the rightful jurisdiction of Texas; that Fillmore appeared resolute in continuing that occupation under the cloak of fulfilling pledges made in Article IX; and that these actions could not be anything but prejudicial and detrimental to Texas.

Both sides made their cases in congress based on their respective interpretations of the Texas annexation resolutions, Articles V and IX of the Treaty of Guadalupe Hidalgo, and other documentary evidence. Each side believed it possessed the better argument and defended its position adamantly. Debate as they most passionately might, however, members of congress on neither side

---

[39] Richardson, comp., *Messages,* Vol. 5, pp. 71-73; *House Exec. Docs.,* 31 Cong., 1 sess., 82 (serial 579), pp. 10-11.
[40] *Cong. Globe,* 31 Cong., 1 sess., App. pp. 1033, 1119.
[41] *House Exec. Docs.,* 31 Cong., 1 sess., 82 (serial 579), pp. 10-11.

42

could establish an airtight case. Various clauses of documents were vague enough to be interpreted in opposite ways as they applied to the boundary dispute. The ambiguities revealed in the debate may have served to convince some members of congress of the reasonableness of compromise.

The New Mexico-Texas bill ultimately passed by congress did establish a realistic boundary between the two polities. In the final fashioning of the settlement, probably no principle was more important than *uti possidetis, i.e.*, what area the respective parties actually controlled and occupied. Another important factor in establishing New Mexico jurisdiction east of the Río Grande was the ingrained hostility of New Mexicans to Texas. They feared that, if forced to submit to Texan jurisdiction, unscrupulous Texans would dispossess New Mexicans of their rights and property.

The case of the Doña Ana headright dramatically illustrated this point. New Mexicans also made it abundantly clear that they did not want African slavery extended into New Mexico, although they desired to retain the area's traditional institution of peonage. Horace Greeley in his *New York Tribune* continued in 1850 to stress the theme that the only real chance for the spread of African slavery into the territories lay in the possible recognition by the federal government of the claim by the slave state of Texas to all of New Mexico lying east of the Río Grande.[42]

A final application of the Guadalupe Hidalgo treaty to the New Mexico-Texas boundary dispute involved the attempt by moderate Texans in the fall of 1850 to convince the populace of their state to accept the boundary decided on by congress in the compromise. Texas's pro-slavery radicals continued to demand that Texas reject the compromise plan, even if it brought bloodshed, disunion and civil war. Most Texans were pleased with congress' settlement, however, especially since Texas would receive $10 million to retire its debt in exchange for relinquishing its claim on the upper Río Grande valley.

Texas conducted a popular referendum on the compromise, and proponents and opponents campaigned at public rallies in the state. A pro-compromise member of the Texas congressional delegation, Representative David Kaufman, utilized an interesting tactic to influence Texans to favor the settlement. Ironically, the device used was a version of the Disturnell treaty map, recently cited by Texans in support of their extreme 1836 boundary claim. It was now employed to convince Texans of the benefits of surrendering some of that claim to New Mexico. For a congressional speech on September 3, Representative James McDowell of Virginia had had a map, based on Disturnell's, drawn up to illustrate the New Mexico-Texas situation. Anyone familiar with more recent, accurate maps of the region recognized that this map grossly distorted area and distance in New Mexico and West Texas. But Kaufman observed how those very distortions might be enlisted in securing Texan adherence to the compromise, for the Disturnell map minimized the area given up by Texas to New Mexico—from more than 103 million acres to only 56.45 million according to Robert Creuzbaur, chief draftsman of the Texas General Land Office and an accomplished map maker himself. The map also made the "free soil" of New Mexico appear more distant from and

---

[42] No editor in the nation in 1850 espoused the causes of New Mexico and free labor there as strongly as Horace Greeley in his *Tribune,* a position he had consistently held in previous years. For his editorials on New Mexico, slavery there, the Texas threat, and federal policy and bills pertaining thereto, see *New York Daily Tribune,* Jan. 24, Mar. 19, Apr. 6, 9, 10, 15, 19, May 4, 11, 20, 21, June 4, 18, 19, 21, 25, July 2, 3, 17, 19, 25, 26, Aug. 5, 8, 12, 15, 19, 26, Sep. 9, 10, 11, 1850.

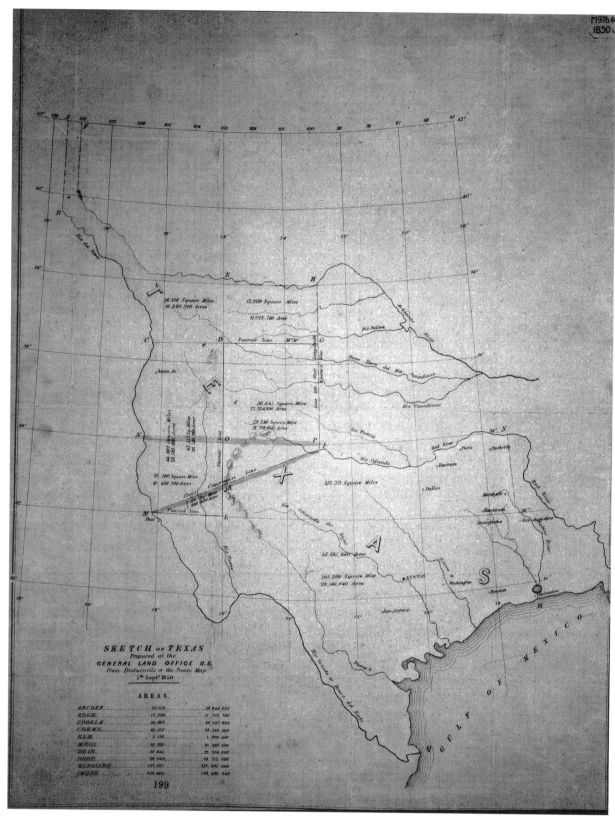

"Kaufman map" (1850), version of Disturnell map.

Courtesy: Center for American History, University of Texas, Austin.

44

thereby less threatening to the settled, slave-holding parts of Texas than it actually is. As Creuzbaur calculated it, San Antonio was in reality eighty-five miles closer to New Mexico than depicted on the map. Kaufman was more interested in appearances than realities, however, in using McDowell's version of the Disturnell map.

With McDowell's permission, Kaufman had the U.S. General Land Office copy the map and then paid lithographer Curtis B. Graham to make a thousand copies of it. Senator Rusk paid for another thousand. These copies were circulated in Texas during the referendum campaign. Critics charged Kaufman with deception in using what became known as the "Kaufman map" as a propaganda tool, but he denied any intent to deceive and blamed the map's errors on the U.S. General Land Office. The popular vote in Texas went overwhelmingly in favor of the compromise (9439 to 3418) and would likely have gone that way without the Kaufman map.[43]

In the various ways described above, the Treaty of Guadalupe Hidalgo and its attached Disturnell map were relevant to the New Mexico-Texas boundary dispute and its final settlement. The foundations of the State of New Mexico and the early history of Doña Ana County were intimately connected with the treaty of 1848 and the Compromise of 1850. This episode was also part of the developing sectional crisis in the ante-bellum United States. New Mexico and Doña Ana County played a significant role in the framing of the last great sectional compromise between north and south prior to the Civil War.

---

[43] Stegmaier, *Texas, New Mexico,* pp. 304-306, 311.

APPENDIX

THE DOÑA ANA PROTEST AGAINST THE MAJOR STEEN HEADRIGHT MARCH 12, 1850

1) ORIGINAL VERSION IN SPANISH:

Señor Gobernador del Territorio del Nuevo Méjico

Los vecinos del Pueblo de Doña Anna CC. [Ciudadanos] hoy de los E.U. [Estados Unidos] y los CC. Mejicanos que retienen sus propiedades conforme á los tratados, en el dho. punto de Doña Anna elevan ante V.S. [Vuestra Señoría] con la mayor sumisión y respeto la queja de que unos comisionados de tejas que arreglan la jurisdicción politica en estos puntos han hecho venta de un billete de terrenos al Major Steen de la guarnición militar de esta plasa en la suma de 75 pesos según unos dicen, y otros en la de setecientos, y el cual ha tomado en tamaño de una legua sobre las fabricas de este mismo Pueblo y los terrenos labrados que las inundan en gran porción. El hecho Señor es tan remarcable que de [desde] luego hace resaltar la injusticia que con apariencias se intento cubrir. Y el hecho es contra lo convenido espresamente en los tratados celebrados entre los E.U. de America y los de Méjico. Es contra el derecho natural y contra el de gentes. Esta conducta nos inspira desconfianza por que contraria las proclamaciones de seguridad y confianza que se nos preconiza. La proclamación del Gral. Kerne [Gen. Kearny] asegura á los habitantes de los puntos que ocupó en la guerra que nos propiedades adquiridas hasta aquella fecha serían respetadas, pues no podía desconocer ni aun el sagrado derecho de primer poseedor, mucho menos adquirida conforme con las leyes. Por ocho años hemos expuesto nuestra existencia e interéses en medio del furor del salvaje que tanto aun nos hostiliza. Resistimos la hambre y las intemperies como no debe desconocer son consiguientes en estos trabajos. Y hombres rodeadas de miserias, que triste Señor sería que se nos arrebatan en el seno de la confianza el fruto de nuestras fatigas. ?Quien por que no hay leyes no estamos en sociedad. Basta lo espuesto á la penetración de V.S. para que no se nos imparta la justicia que nos asista resolviendo si tenemos derecho á estas propiedades, para que no se nos molesta, ni prive de los goces que esperamos baja los auspicios de las leyes libres que nos rigen y garantizan positivamente nuestras vidas y propiedades. Que esta sea el escudo que rechase semejantes atentados que no esperamos ver repetir, por la probidad que le adorna, Con la más humilde confianza nos ofrecemos y esperamos la resolución de V.S.

Doña Anna   Marzo 12 de 1850.

Guadalupe Miranda (rubrica)*

A.B. Rohmann (rubrica)

Toniha García (rubrica)

Bautista Montoya (rubrica)

Bernabe Montoya +

Juan José Carrera (rubrica)

Epitacio Barela +
Miguel Montoya (rubrica)
José María Flores +
José __?__ García (rubrica)
Lorenzio Espalin (rubrica)
Lucíano Labade (rubrica)
Rumaldo Sedios +
José Nebares (rubrica)
Geronimo Lujan (rubrica)
Monico Benabides (rubrica)
Juan José Benabides (rubrica)
Manuel Lucero +
Luz Prado (rubrica)
José Alejandro Maldonado (rubrica)
Guadalupe Olivares (rubrica)
Francisco Sedillo +
Juan Mª Ponce León (rubrica)
José Mª Rodriguez (rubrica)
Rafael Ruelas (rubrica)
Florentino Estrada (rubrica)
Buenav^{ra} Zamora +
Fran^{co} Jamarillo (rubrica)
Fran^{co} Rodriguez (rubrica)
Jesuis Madrid +
Gregorio Davalos (rubrica)
Fran^{co} Velarde (rubrica)
José Telles +
Manuel Lusero +
Jesus Muñoz
Fran^{co} Bario (rubrica)
Antonio Herrera +
Dario Serna (rubrica)
Justo Barela +
Juan Felipe Rodriguez +
Adan Lopes +
Luciano Rael (rubrica)
Pablo Melendres (rubrica)
Bicente Garrcia (rubrica)
Felipe Madrid +

* A *rubrica* (rubric) was a decorative flourish at the end of a signature indicating that the person was literate enough to write his own name. Persons who had someone else sign for them placed crosses after their names, as above.

2) CONTEMPORARY ENGLISH VERSION:*

To his Excellency the Governor of the Territory of New Mexico

The citizens of the town of Doña Ana, and now citizens of the United States; in union with citizens of Mexico who hold property agreeable to the treaty in said town of Doña Ana respectfully represent to your Excellency with the greatest submission and respect the complaint that some Texas commissioners that regulated the Political jurisdiction in this place and vicinity, have sold a land warrant or certificate to Maj. Steen the military commander of this place in the sum of seventy five dollars as some say and others in seven hundred with which he has taken one league of land including the houses of the town and the cultivated lands and a grand portion of the adjoining lands—the Act Sir! is so remarkable that it at once shows the injustice which with appearances it wishes to cover. The Act Sir! is so directly contrary to the Treaty entered into between the United States of America and the Republic of Mexico. It is contrary to all natural right and contrary to that of the people. This conduct makes us mistrust because it is contrary to the proclamation of security and protection which has been promised us. The proclamation of Gen Carny [Kearny] assured to the inhabitants of this and other places that he occupied during the war, that their property acquired up to that date should be respected because the sacred right of the first owner could not be denied much less the right of property acquired by law. We have occupied this place exposed for eight years our existence and property in the midst of the fury of the Savage[s] who even yet molest us We have resisted hunger and the vicissitudes which should not be denied, that always follow in these troubles. And men surrounded with miseries, how unfortunate it would be to wrest from the bosom of confidence, the fruits of their toils For whom are there no social laws? But it is sufficient what we have already represented to your Excellency that you may grant us justice and also to assist you in resolving whether or not our claim is just to this property, So that we may not be molested nor deprived of the enjoyments that we expect under the protection of the liberal laws that govern us and guarantee positively our lives & property That this may be the shield to protect us from such attempts which we hope not to repeat. Knowing the probity with which you are adorned with the most humble confidence we submit ourselves and await the resolution of Your Excellency.

Doña Ana   March 12th 1850

*The transcription of the handwritten Spanish document, slightly edited here, was provided by a collaboration of Dr. Teresa Lubrano of Cameron University and Dr. John P. Wilson and Dr. Rick Hendricks of Las Cruces, New Mexico. The handwritten original in Spanish and the contemporary English version (not a literal translation) are found with Munroe to Jones, May 20, 1850, cited above.

MALCOLM EBRIGHT

The year of 1998 marks the entry into New Mexico four hundred years ago of Spanish and Mexican Indian settlers led by Spanish grandee Don Juan de Oñate. With the entry of the Spanish came the introduction of a complex of cultures and traditions not familiar to the native peoples. The concept of land grants was one such new custom. At the discretion of those in power either in Mexico or in Spain, tracts of land were granted to a select number of people.

Land grants which never should have been awarded, land obtained by suspected and proven forgery, claims unsupported by valid evidence, and the drama of the Court of Private Land Claims—it all happened in New Mexico over a hundred years ago. The complexity of the land-claim disputes was magnified by an ongoing debate over water rights. Before and after the Treaty of Guadalupe Hidalgo, lawsuits were filed disputing the ownership of land and water rights.

Over a century later, land-grant conflicts are not strangers to our present-day legal system. Land disputes, revived by heirs and alleged heirs of the *antepasados* who claim their rights to grants, inevitably end up in the courts. Unsettled land claims are filed in court as a last resort to determine who truly owns the land. It is as if the scripts of those who argued before the Court of Private Land Claims years ago are periodically discovered, dusted, and handed to the next generation of land-grant attorneys. However, at the rate that these disputes are resolved, the legal struggles to determine the rightful ownership of much land in New Mexico may well continue through the next generation.

Recently, I was privileged to meet a fascinating individual whose passion for New Mexico history was instantly visible in his eyes and in his book of essays, *Land Grants and Lawsuits in Northern New Mexico,* first published in 1994. Malcolm Ebright, a historian and attorney, is not easily forgotten. He stands tall and impressive, slightly long silvery blond hair tied back loosely in a not-so-organized fashion. His ponytail brings back memories of the "anti-establishment" movement of the sixties.

An air of distinction surrounds Malcolm Ebright. At first sight and without words, Ebright commands respect and recognition. He is a man whose words become action and whose actions are evidence of his character as a fine historian and a man committed to his cause. His youthful spirit complements his curious mind. For years, Ebright has explored the history of New Mexico land grants and water rights.

In his work Ebright weaves the lives of colorful characters into his studies of land-grant history in New Mexico. An example is the speculating priest from Saint Louis, Missouri, Thomas Aquinas

Hayes, known in northern New Mexico as Tomás de Aquino, who acquired a reputation of questionable character and was arrested in Albuquerque on a warrant from Colorado. As a buyer and seller of grants, this priest made a 2,400 percent profit from his sale of the Ramon Vigil Grant.

Ebright's passion for justice is visible in his written word and was displayed clearly in his oral presentation on February 28, 1998, at the Doña Ana County Historical Society symposium on the Treaty of Guadalupe Hidalgo. As an attorney, Ebright demonstrates his sensitivity to the unequal standing faced by many parties in their challenges to the government over water and land issues.

Through his research, Ebright has uncovered surprising incidents of unethical practices by government officials and other individuals charged with fiduciary duties. Most importantly, he has courageously brought forth to the public extremely controversial and, sometimes, emotionally painful issues. Perhaps as more of us learn our own histories and reevaluate our pasts, we will have the wisdom to apply what we learn and continue to learn to a reconciliation of the wrongs our *antepasados* suffered and sometimes inflicted. If we have not yet begun to do so, perhaps now, during the four hundred-year anniversary celebration of the entry of the Spanish, is a good time to begin. I thank and appreciate Malcolm Ebright for his challenging findings. I encourage us all to read his essay below and his other works, and to continue to strive for equality and dignity for all peoples.

Beatriz Valadez Ferreira
Las Cruces, New Mexico

LAND GRANT ADJUDICATION IN NEW MEXICO

UNDER THE TREATY OF GUADALUPE HIDALGO

Malcolm Ebright

Negotiating treaties is the business of diplomats. It is the business of drawing lines on a map after conquest has readjusted the areas of dominion. The business of implementing those treaties is the work of surveyors and boundary commissioners who mark the boundary lines on the ground. But most important is the business of protecting the property rights of those who have stayed put while new lines of sovereignty were drawn around them. This is the business that the Treaty of Guadalupe Hidalgo failed to accomplish, which still concerns us today. It entails an effort to readjust the patterns of land ownership and land usage that were skewed after the treaty was signed.

Three and a half centuries preceding the Treaty of Guadalupe Hidalgo, the first boundary line was drawn in the New World. During the summer of 1492, shortly after the first of Columbus's voyages of discovery, Pope Alexander VI drew a vertical line on the map of the New World: everything west of the line belonged to Spain, everything east of the line was owned by Portugal.[1] In spite of arguments by theologians like Bartolomé de las Casas about the right of kings, queens and the pope to divide and subjugate the indigenous population of the Americas, the line stuck.[2] It took more than three hundred years of negotiation and diplomacy to actually locate the line on the ground. Ever since, this line has separated Portuguese-speaking Brazil from the Spanish-speaking countries of South America. Drawing the final line required a new treaty (Treaty of San Ildefonso, 1777) and a joint Spanish-Portuguese Boundary Commission. But the rights of the indigenous people who had these boundary lines drawn around them are still being negotiated.[3]

Similarly, 350 years later, Mexico and the United States drew a roughly horizontal line which now separates the two countries, in spite of debate over United States's justification for its war of expansion and conquest. Again, because of spectacular errors in the Disturnell map (in terms of

---

[1] Clarence H. Haring, *The Spanish Empire in America* (New York: Harcourt, Brace, Jovanovich, 1947), p. 7. The papal bull *Inter Castera,* promulgated between May and September 1492, divided the New World between Spain and Portugal. The Treaty of Tordesillas between Castile and Portugal in 1494 established the Line of Demarcation between 48 and 49 degrees of longitude west of Greenwich.

[2] Bartolomé de las Casas, *In Defense of the Indians,* Stafford Poole, ed. and trans. (DeKalb: Northern Illinois University Press, 1992), pp. 349-362.

[3] The Tordesillas line was substantially modified to give Portugal the Amazon region as a result of a diplomatic battle over maps. Michael Layland, "Devious Diplomacy," in *Mercator's World,* Vol. 3 (Jan.-Feb. 1998), pp. 16-25. Layland's previous articles in this journal (Vol. 1, nos. 1, 2 and 5) discuss earlier events in the saga of mapping the Tordesillas line. Brazil borders every South American country except Chile and Ecuador.

latitude and longitude, El Paso was shown far north and east of its actual location), a boundary commission and a new treaty were required in order to lay out this still-contested line on the ground.[4]

With the surveyor's exactitude, the boundary line between Mexico and the United States has been fixed and monumented. But do we understand with the same precision the larger meaning of the Treaty of Guadalupe Hidalgo, and how its promises were broken?

This treaty is both the most important document in the history of relations between Mexico and the United States and the most misunderstood. In commemorating the one-hundred and fiftieth anniversary of the signing and ratification of the treaty, it is my hope that some of this misunderstanding can be dispelled, and that this occasion can mark the beginning of a new effort to raise the Treaty of Guadalupe Hidalgo beyond the level of an agreement more honored in the breach than in the observance. Before the treaty can become a document that will be cited by courts as a basis for upholding rights to land and water in the southwest, some misunderstandings surrounding the treaty need to be examined critically.[5]

The most difficult thing for Hispanic New Mexicans to understand in connection with the Treaty of Guadalupe Hidalgo is the expectation that by negotiating and signing it the United States was promising New Mexicans that their property would be protected in accordance with clear legal standards as to which rights were valid. In addition, New Mexicans who unfairly lost land or water rights protected by the treaty thought they had possibility of redress in U.S. courts. This myth grew from the idea that the promises made by the United States were enforceable. How it might be dispelled will be discussed by reviewing, first, the negotiation of the property rights guaranteed in the treaty; second, what was left of these guarantees when the U.S. Senate deleted Article X from the treaty; and third, how the treaty might have been applied to New Mexico land grants and water rights. I will review two New Mexico land grants to test whether they were fairly adjudicated under the treaty: the Baca Floats, that arose out of the Las Vegas Grant, and the Embudo Grant.

I. Negotiation of the Treaty

The negotiation of the Treaty of Guadalupe Hidalgo took place as the invasion of central Mexico by the U.S. Army under General Winfield Scott was taking place. Attached to Scott's army was the commissioner empowered by the United States to negotiate with Mexico, Nicholas Trist. A man described as snobbish, defiant, charming and idealistic, he was sent to Mexico by President James K. Polk (and his Secretary of State, James Buchanan) with a draft treaty that was to be the basis of negotiations with Mexico. This draft, which Trist brought to Mexico in a sealed container and officiously directed General Winfield Scott to forward to Mexican authorities, contained eleven

---

[4] Odie B. Faulk, *Too Far North ... Too Far South: The Controversial Boundary Survey and the Epic Story of the Gadsden Purchase* (Los Angeles: Westernlore Press, 1967); and Paul Neff Garber, *The Gadsden Treaty* (Gloucester, MA: Peter Smith, 1959).

[5] Recent scholarship on the treaty includes Richard Griswold, del Castillo, *The Treaty of Guadalupe Hidalgo: A Legacy of Conflict* (Norman: University of Oklahoma Press, 1990); Fernando Chacon Gómez, "The Intended and Actual Effects of Article VIII of the Treaty of Guadalupe Hidalgo: Mexican Treaty Rights under International and Domestic Law" (Ph.D. diss., University of Michigan, 1966); and Geoffrey P. Mawn, "A Land-Grant Guarantee: The Treaty of Guadalupe Hidalgo or the Protocol of Querétaro," in *Journal of the West,* Vol. 14 (Oct. 1975), pp. 49-63.

articles, none of which made any mention of guaranteeing land grants.[6] However, Trist was instructed not to object if the Mexican government requested such a guarantee. On August 27, 1847, during an armistice called to allow for peace negotiations, the Mexican commissioners proposed the first provision specifically dealing with Spanish and Mexican land grants in any U.S. treaty. It provided that land grants made by Mexico "shall be valid and permanent, and shall be sustained and guarded by the government of the United States." This was the beginning of what would become Article X of the treaty eventually signed by Trist and the Mexican commissioners at the villa of Guadalupe Hidalgo on February 2, 1848.[7]

After this initial exchange, negotiations were suspended when the two-week armistice was terminated. General Scott resumed his attack on Mexico City, and on September 14, 1847, the American army occupied the capital. With the capture of Mexico City a new phase of negotiations began, during which Trist received word that he had been recalled and ordered to return to Washington. After reporting his recall to the Mexican government on November 24, and his intention to depart, Trist reflected on how much progress toward agreement had been achieved, and on December 4 he decided to remain in Mexico to finish the job.

Final, secret negotiations began again on January 2, 1848, in the villa of Guadalupe Hidalgo near Mexico City, ending with the signing of the treaty a month later. Throughout these negotiations the threat of further occupation of Mexico by General Scott was palpable. Scott received reinforcements on January 22, and on January 29 the Mexican government was notified that these forces would advance further into the interior of Mexico unless a treaty of peace were signed. It was during this period of hurried negotiations that the final versions of the land-grant guarantees in the treaty were negotiated.[8]

During these last-ditch negotiations the Mexican commissioners proposed a new draft of what was to become Article X. Substantially the same as the draft of August 27, it stated that land grants made by Mexico were "valid and subsisting and should be supported and observed by the United States." In other words, the United States would confirm all land grants made by Mexico. Trist responded that this language was not feasible because it would validate all land grants whether or not their conditions had been fulfilled. Accordingly, Trist drafted substitute language which became part of Article X in the treaty. It provided that land grants "shall be respected as valid, to the same extent that the same grants would be valid if the said territories had remained within the limits of Mexico ... ."[9]

---

[6] Wallace Ohrt, *Defiant Peacemaker: Nicholas Trist in the Mexican War,* The Elma Dill Russell Spencer Series in the West and Southwest, No. 17 (College Station: Texas A&M University Press, 1997), pp. 163-167.

[7] For Trist's instructions and the draft treaty received when he was appointed commissioner on April 15, 1847, see Hunter Miller, ed., *Treaties and Other International Acts of the United States of America* (Washington: Government Printing Office, 1937), Vol. 5, pp. 262-267. For the instructions given to the Mexican commissioners and the Mexican draft treaty see *ibid.,* pp. 299-302.

[8] George L. Rives, *The United States and Mexico, 1821-1848* (orig. ed. 1913; reprinted New York: Krause Reprint Co., 1969), pp. 500-566; Miller, *Treaties,* Vol. V, pp. 289-293, 296-297, 314-315.

[9] For a discussion of Article X and the genesis of various portions of it, see Mawn, "Land-Grant Guarantee," pp. 42-55.

Thus, the test of the validity of Mexican and also Spanish land grants was whether they were valid under Mexican law and practice. In fact, such a standard, testing which grants should be confirmed by the United States and which ones rejected, is also contained in international law. It represents a reasonable basis for judging fairness in the confirmation of property rights under the treaty. If this criterion had been applied to land-grant adjudication in New Mexico, we would not have the distorted picture we now see, where valid land grants were rejected and grants were confirmed which would have been nonexistent or faulty under Mexican law and custom. On the map of New Mexico those rejected grants are now U.S. government land, administered by the U.S. Forest Service or the Bureau of Land Management, while the improperly confirmed grants are now valuable private property.

How then did this most important article of the treaty get eliminated? When the treaty signed at Guadalupe Hidalgo reached Washington, DC, it was met with conflicting views depending on politics. Secretary of State Buchanan had initially opposed any land acquisition. He then became involved with preparing the treaty draft which Trist took to Mexico. By the time the signed treaty reached Washington for ratification, he had come to believe that *more* territory should be demanded of Mexico. Polk believed that Buchanan's change of heart was based on his candidacy for president, as a nod toward persons who favored annexation of all of Mexico. Polk himself, in the last year of his presidency, had lost the support of many Americans, who now wanted an end to a war that had become an embarrassment. The president was angry with Trist for his "arrogant, imprudent" actions in defying the order to return to Washington. But Polk could also see that most of his initial objectives for the negotiations had been achieved. So the president called a meeting of his cabinet. Over the objections of Buchanan and Secretary of the Treasury Robert J. Walker, Polk sided with the four members of the cabinet who favored sending the treaty to the senate. The only modification suggested was outright deletion of Article X. After intense debate in the senate, the treaty was ratified on March 10, 1848, with the deletion of Article X and revision of objectionable parts of several other articles.[10]

Article X appeared to be a pawn that was sacrificed in order to get the treaty approved at the time. But Secretary of State Buchanan explained a few months later that the deletion was based on objection to the part of Article X that provided additional time for grantees to fulfill conditions of their grants that had not been met.

Without Article X, the strongest property-rights guarantee was found in Article VIII, but a mistranslation of that article has weakened its effect. Article VIII contains the oft-repeated language that property of Mexican citizens "shall be inviolably respected." The mistranslation makes it appear that this guarantee flows only to Mexican citizens "not established there [in New Mexico]," so that the actual inhabitants of the newly acquired U.S. territory would not receive the benefits of Article VIII. A review of an earlier draft of the treaty makes it clear, however, that the drafters of this article

[10] For a review of Senate proceedings leading to ratification and Polk's message to the Senate, see Miller, *Treaties,* Vol. 5, pp. 246-253. For a brief discussion of reasons for deleting Article X see Mawn, "Land-Grant Guarantee," p. 54. See also Ohrt, *Defiant Peacemaker,* pp. 147-150.

were concerned about guaranteeing property rights to three classes of Mexican citizens: those who elected to leave New Mexico and retain their Mexican citizenship; those who elected to stay in New Mexico and retain their Mexican citizenship; and those who elected to stay in New Mexico and become American citizens.

This concern with carefully defining the classes of Mexican citizens whose property would be protected is found in the first two paragraphs of Article VIII. The first paragraph discusses the options to continue to reside in New Mexico or to leave, and the second paragraph relates to the citizenship options of persons who remain in New Mexico. Then the third paragraph guarantees property rights of all three classes: "The property of all classes [of individuals] living in the said territory, and that [property] now belonging to Mexicans not living there, shall be inviolably respected."[11] This translation would avoid the incongruous conclusion that the "inviolably respected" language applies only to the class of Mexican citizens who decided not to stay in New Mexico.[12]

It was the Mexican commissioners who submitted the language of what became Article VIII. Article IX of the draft treaty offered to Trist on January 9, 1848, contained a simplified version of Article VIII of the final treaty. In that draft the three classes of inhabitants are delineated, then the final sentence of the paragraph contains the property guarantee that corresponds to the last paragraph of Article VIII: "but in every case, they and their property shall enjoy the most ample guaranty." This makes clear the intention of the Mexican commissioners to establish three classes of Mexican citizens and provide protection for the property of all members of each class.[13]

The Mexican draft treaty submitted on January 9 was in Spanish, but the only copy we have is a "hurried" translation by Edward Thornton, a member of the British legation in Mexico City who had assisted in the treaty negotiations from the beginning. The original of this Mexican draft was returned to the Mexican commissioners by Trist with suggested modifications noted on it.[14] Then negotiations intensified, from January 13-25, leading to an agreement in principle on January 25. The Mexican commissioners amplified the text of what became Article VIII, and Trist added language to the article of the draft treaty that became Article X. Even when the treaty was signed on February 2, it probably was not in final form. Since Article VIII had been drafted and amplified by the Mexican commissioners, the Spanish version must have come first and the mistranslation would have been Trist's.

---

[11] Miller, *Treaties,* Vol. 5, pp. 210-211. See Appendix A for both the Spanish and English of Article VIII as presently translated, and Appendix B for Article VIII under the new translation.

[12] Some scholars have accepted the existing translation of Article VIII at face value. Griswold del Castillo, *Treaty,* pp. 62-63: "*Absentee* landholders would have their property 'inviolably respected,' and others would 'be maintained and protected in the free enjoyment of their liberty and property.'" Other scholars have misread the mistranslation. Mawn, "Land-Grant Guarantee," p. 60: "the [land-grant] guarantee specifically is contained in the wording and spirit of one paragraph of Article VIII of the treaty which states: 'In the said territories, property of every kind, now belonging to the Mexicans *now* established there, shall be inviolably respected'" (emphasis mine).

[13] Miller, *Treaties,* Vol. 5, p. 311. See Appendix C for Articles 8, 9, 10 and 11 of the Mexican draft treaty submitted on Jan. 9, 1848.

[14] Miller, *Treaties,* Vol. 5, p. 309. On Edward Thornton see Rives, *U.S. and Mexico,* pp. 440-447, 489, 594-601.

II. Interpretation of the Treaty

The basic rules of how treaties should be construed by the courts should help resolve any doubts as to how the Spanish version should be evaluated. When a treaty is executed in two languages, both versions are deemed to be originals. This principal was crucial in the U.S. Supreme Court's 1833 decision in *U.S. v. Percheman,*[15] where John Marshall reversed a decision he had made four years earlier. Construing the same language in the Florida treaty dealing with land grants, Marshall relied on the English version of the treaty in the first case but, in *Percheman,* he relied on the Spanish version. Percheman's attorney argued that key language in the English version had been mistranslated and Justice Marshall agreed.[16]

Several other rules of construction argue for the new translation of the Spanish version of Article VIII of the Treaty of Guadalupe Hidalgo. One such rule says that, where there are two possible constructions, one restrictive of rights claimed under the treaty and the other more favorable to those rights, the liberal construction should prevail.[17] In addition, every treaty is to be interpreted in light of the circumstances existing at the time it was entered into, including the history of the negotiations and diplomatic correspondence of involved parties. Thus, Article IX of the draft treaty submitted by Mexico, which comports with the new translation, should be given great weight.[18] In addition, the fact that the Mexican commissioners were particularly concerned with the rights of its citizens who lived in ceded territory, according to Trist, argues powerfully for the interpretation that would not ignore those inhabitants, as the current translation does.

III. Application of the Treaty by Congress and the Courts

The first test of how the treaty would be applied to land grants came in 1851 in California which, already admitted to statehood, established a commission to adjudicate land grants there. The commission was instructed that, in deciding on the validity of land grants, it was to be governed in part by the Treaty of Guadalupe Hidalgo.[19] But when the first test case came before the U.S. Supreme Court challenging the California procedure as being in violation of the treaty, the court held that this was not a legal issue that the courts could decide. The court did not even examine the provisions of the treaty since, under its ruling, the only remedy left to the plaintiff was political: to get the government of Mexico to raise the issue with the United States. The Supreme Court said that, if the plaintiffs' rights under the treaty were violated by the California statute, "it was a matter of international concern, which the two states [Mexico and the United States] must determine by [a new] treaty, or by such means as enables one state to enforce upon another the obligations of treaty."[20]

---

[15] *U.S. v. Percheman,* 32 U.S. 50, 87-88 (183). *American Jurisprudence,* 2d ed. (Jurisprudence publisher, 1974), Vol. 74, pp. 847-848; Malcolm Ebright, *Land Grants and Lawsuits in Northern New Mexico* (Albuquerque: University of New Mexico Press, 1994), pp. 31-32.

[16] The earlier case was *Foster v. Nelson* 27 U.S. 253 (1829). The language in question was "[land grants] *quedarán ratificadas y reconocidas a las personas que estan en posesión de ellas....*" The word "quedarán" was translated "shall be" in the first case, and "remain" in *Percheman.*

[17] *American Jurisprudence,* Vol. 74, pp. 843-845.

[18] *Ibid.,* p. 848.

[19] An act to ascertain and settle the private land claims in the State of California, Sec. 11.

[20] *Botiller v. Dominguez,* 130 U.S. 238 (1888).

The legislation establishing the New Mexico Surveyor General and Court of Private Land Claims also referred to the Treaty of Guadalupe Hidalgo, but it was the surveyor general statute that best defined and clarified the nature of the land-grant guarantee contained in the treaty after deletion of Article X. Section 8 of that legislation orders the surveyor general to "make a full report ... [of all claims] with his decision as to the validity ... under the laws usages and customs of the country *before* its cession to the United States."[21] Congress was apparently satisfied, even after all the obfuscation about whether the Protocol of Querétaro correctly interpreted the effect of the treaty,[22] that the test for validity of a land grant was whether it was valid under Mexican law, practice and custom. This test of land-grant validity was reiterated in instructions given by the General Land Office in Washington to William Pelham, the first Surveyor General of New Mexico, shortly before he left for Santa Fé. John Wilson, G.L.O. Commissioner, instructed Pelham that the U.S. government was obliged "to deal with private land titles ... precisely as Mexico would have done had the sovereignty not changed. We are bound to recognize all titles, as she would have done ... ."[23]

This test of validity, if rigorously applied, would have forced rejection of many land grants that were confirmed improperly, and would have compelled confirmation of many hundreds of thousand acres of land-grant lands that were wrongfully rejected.

IV. Application of the Treaty to Land Grants in New Mexico

The issue of land-grant validity was confused by the fact that it was seldom raised in a comprehensive fashion in a broad historical context, but instead was debated by lawyers in relation to numerous specific land grants. During the surveyor general period, 1854-1891, prior to the establishment of the Court of Private Land Claims, there was little debate about the validity of land grants made under Spain and Mexico. Instead the surveyors general, with little or no background in the law or in the history of Spain and Mexico, made decisions as to land-grant validity. Then congress, with even less background and understanding of the issues, often gave rubber-stamp approvals to surveyor general decisions.[24]

The basic requirements for a valid land grant under Spain and Mexico were simply a grant by the governor evidenced by written documents, plus some form of settlement on the land. While there were some exceptions, without these two fundamental elements there could be no valid grant under either Spain or Mexico. If either of these requirements was lacking, a grantee might seek a revalidation of a defective grant from the governor, thus curing the defect if the governor made the

---

[21] An Act to establish the offices of Surveyor General of New Mexico, Kansas and Nebraska. 10 *U.S. Statutes* 308-310.

[22] For a discussion of the Protocol of Querétaro see Mawn, "Land-Grant Guarantee," pp. 54-61.

[23] Instructions, G.L.O. Comr. John Wilson to Surveyor Gen. William Pelham. Sen. Misc. Doc. No. 12, 42d Cong., 1st sess. (1871), pp. 1-7, cited in J.J. Bowden, "Private Land Claims in the Southwest" (M.A. thesis, Southern Methodist University, 1969), pp. 176-180.

[24] In 1860 the U.S. House of Representatives Committee on Private Land Claims recommended that a commission replace the surveyor general "whose fitness for surveying is not supposed to qualify him particularly for discharging the duties of a judge." The committee further stated that "it has not time to scrutinize ... the application as made by the Surveyor General of the Spanish and Mexican laws and usages...." H.R. Report No. 321, 36 Cong., 1st sess., 1-2 (1860), cited in Ebright, *The Tierra Amarilla Grant: A History of Chicanery* (Santa Fe: Center for Land Grant Studies, 1993), p. 22.

new grant. Often what would happen in the case of a defective grant would be a request from another prospective grantee for the same land. If the second petition were granted, the new grant would supersede the old one. These principles were found in the 17th-century *Recopilación de leyes de los reynos de las Indias,* the Mexican colonization law of 1828, and in the practice of the governments of Spain and Mexico over a period at least 150 years.[25]

When the United States applied these principles of land-grant validity to the Mexican period, at least five outcomes resulted. Some valid grants were rejected entirely (Embudo); some valid grants were partially rejected (San Joaquín, San Miguel del Bado); some valid grants were confirmed to the wrong people (Tierra Amarilla); some valid grants were confirmed to the right people (Truchas, Tecolote); and some invalid grants were confirmed (Sebastián de Vargas, the Baca Locations). It is only in the case where valid grants were confirmed to the right claimants that it could be said truly that justice was done. In order to see the effects of the injustice that was done in the other situations, try to visualize a map of New Mexico and its variety of property ownership under Mexico before the Treaty of Guadalupe Hidalgo and under the United States shortly after the treaty was signed. Visualize the public domain of both countries as green, private property as red, and the common lands of community grants as yellow. The amount of private property shown in red would be about the same on both maps. The biggest difference would be the community property which would be vastly reduced on the U.S. map due to the rejection of the common lands of many valid community grants. Almost all of what would be yellow under Mexico would have changed to green on the U.S. map.

We shall now examine two cases that illustrate some of these categories. The so-called Baca Floats exemplify invalid grants that were confirmed as private property, turning 500,000 acres of what was green under Mexico to red under the United States. Another example in this category is the Sebastián de Vargas Grant south of Santa Fé. In both cases Mexican public domain was privatized so that what had been used by everyone without charge became concentrated in the hands of a few entrepreneurs who were then able to reap handsome profits for themselves.[26]

The case study of the Embudo Grant illustrates the category of a valid grant rejected in its entirety; the San Miguel del Bado Grant exemplifies a valid grant partially rejected. In both cases what was yellow under Mexico became green under the United States. In all four cases common lands were either completely lost or became more regulated and subject to outside control. The resulting distortion of the property map of New Mexico was the direct result of the failure of U.S. courts or congress to decide these cases as Mexican authorities would have done. The most flagrant example is the Baca Locations arising from the Cabesa de Baca Grant.

---

[25] Reglamento de 21 de Noviembre de 1828 para la colonización de los Territorios, in Francisco de la Maza, *Código de Colonización y Terrenos Baldios de la República Mexicana* (México, 1893); *Recopilación de leyes de los reynos de las Indias* (Madrid: Iulian de Paredes, 1681).

[26] Portions of the Sebastián de Vargas Grant are in the hands of a private developer as this is written, and the owners of Baca Location No. 1 are negotiating with the U.S. Forest Service for a purchase by the U.S. government which would turn 100,000 acres of private land back to public domain.

V. The Baca Locations

Luís María Cabesa de Baca owned land at Peña Blanca and applied for a land grant in the Las Vegas area of New Mexico to graze his large sheep herd. Although there were several questionable factors about the request, Cabesa de Baca received the grant in 1821 of a tract containing almost 500,000 acres. Over the next ten years he remained in Peña Blanca while his sons and a few shepherds tried to occupy the grant. Settlement on the grant was sporadic due to Indian raids. By the early 1830s Luís María and his sons (who by then had shortened their name to Baca) were forced to abandon the grant.[27]

At about the same time as the Baca Grant was abandoned, population pressure at San Miguel del Bado, together with scarcity of agricultural land and irrigation water, led to a second petition for the same land covered by the 1821 Baca Grant. This petition was on behalf of about thirty families who told the governor that they needed farming lands to support their families and that this land was public domain *(terreno baldío)*. In 1835 Governor Francisco Sarracino made the Las Vegas community land grant to the petitioners and anyone else who lacked farming lands. Members of the Baca family were among those who received allotments and settled under this Las Vegas Grant. But soon after the Surveyor General of New Mexico office was established *two* claims were filed for the land covered by that grant, one by the Baca heirs and the other by the Las Vegas community land grant.[28]

Surveyor General Pelham had been in office for only a few months when he was called upon to decide between the Las Vegas Grant and the claim of the Baca heirs. The cases were consolidated, and after a lengthy hearing Pelham found both grants to be valid! For some reason, this first surveyor general thought that he did not have the power to adjudicate title disputes between opposing claims, so he recommended that congress confirm both claims, leaving it to "the proper tribunals" to decide. Pelham failed to explain how his decision comported with his instructions to validate land grants in accordance with Mexican law and custom, "to recognize all titles, as she [Mexico] would have done." By the time the thorny question reached the senate Committee on Private Lands, John Watt, attorney for the Baca heirs, had made the government an offer it could not refuse. The Baca heirs would relinquish their title claim to the Las Vegas Grant if they were given an equivalent amount of land elsewhere in the territory. The committee recommended acceptance of the offer, stating that the proposal was a means of avoiding future litigation and "would undoubtedly have been acceded to by Mexico if the Territory had remained hers."[29]

---

[27] Among the questionable aspects of the Cabesa de Baca Grant was that the petition for the grant was directed to the provincial deputation of Durango instead of the governor of New Mexico. Also, Cabesa de Baca's Peña Blanca ranch had been acquired from Cochití Pueblo which claimed that Baca had used intimidation and fraud to induce certain pueblo members to sell the land to him. A lawsuit filed by Cochití was decided in the pueblo's favor, but Baca refused to vacate the property. Charles Cutter, *The Protector de Indios in Colonial New Mexico, 1659-1821* (Albuquerque: University of New Mexico Press, 1986), pp. 88-92; Luís María Cabesa de Baca Grant, NM Land Grants-Surveyor General Office (microfilm, NMLG-SG), Roll 14, frames 1103-06; Roll 15, fr. 30-34; Ebright, *Land Grants,* pp. 174-178.

[28] NMLG-SG, Roll 15, fr. 7-16; Ebright, *Land Grants,* pp. 178-182, 204.

[29] U.S. Senate Report No. 228, 36 Cong., 1st sess., p. 3 (1860); Bowden, "Private Land Claims," Vol. 3, pp. 786-787, 797-798.

While this arrangement was supposed to be a means of avoiding litigation, it led to encroachment on a valid grant in Arizona, two lawsuits, and an additional act of congress. The senate committee at least made some attempt to follow the mandate to "do what Mexico would have done," but Article X had said that land grants would be valid if valid under Mexico. This was a signal to observe what New Mexico officials *did* at the time these grants were made, and to reconstruct what Mexico's law and custom dictated regarding land-grant validity prior to 1848. If the surveyor general had examined the Las Vegas Community Grant documents carefully, he would have noted that when the petition was referred to the San Miguel del Bado *ayuntamiento* for its opinion as to whether the land was available for a new grant, the ayuntamiento reported that the land was public domain and that a new grant would not prejudice third parties. The ayuntamiento's finding implied that the grant had been abandoned by 1835. Instead of looking at the evidence in the grant documents from the 1830s, the senate committee blithely stated that Mexico would have done in the 1860s what congress did. This bordered on the absurd. No evidence was given for this speculative view.[30]

When the Las Vegas Grant was surveyed at a little less than 500,000 acres, the Baca heirs were told to pick five tracts of about 100,000 acres each anywhere in the former Territory of New Mexico. This gave the Baca claimants land that was more valuable than that of the Las Vegas Grant since they were able to pick the choicest land in the territory. What the U.S. Congress did in approving this deal was appalling in view of the millions of acres of valid land grants that were rejected. The Baca Floats or Baca Locations, as they are also called, are still controversial.

Although all the chosen five tracts of land were initially in the Territory of New Mexico, two are located in what is now Arizona and one in Colorado. One of the Arizona locations was found to conflict with an 1824 grant to Leon Herreros known as the San José de Sonoita Grant. Even though the Sonoita Grant had been confirmed by the Court of Private Land Claims, the Baca heirs insisted they had a right to the portion of their tract that overlapped the Sonoita Grant, reasoning that the Sonoita claimants had forfeited their rights by not submitting an earlier claim to the Surveyor General. The Baca heirs were able to convince the federal district court of their erroneous position, but were reversed by the Ninth Circuit Court of Appeals, which held that the Sonoita Grant was a perfect grant entitled to protection under the Gadsden Treaty. The court of appeals approved the following statements about treaty protection: "this grant was one which, at the time of the cession in 1853, was recognized by the government of Mexico as valid, and therefore one which it was the duty of this government to respect and enforce," and "this government promised to inviolably respect the property of Mexicans. That means the property as it then was ... ."[31]

This is exactly what the Treaty of Guadalupe Hidalgo and the Gadsden Treaty said, but it was not enunciated by the court of appeals in the 1850s but in 1920. By then the Sonoita heirs had been required to obtain lawyers, both to have the grant confirmed and to defend it in federal court, before they received this protection. The reason they had to fight this conflicting claim was the blindness of the congressional committee that authorized the Baca floats in the first place. That committee had

---

[30] NMLG-SG, Roll 15, fr. 8-9.
[31] *Ely Real Estate and Investment Co. v. Watts,* 252 F. 721, 723.

cavalierly stated that the Baca heirs' offer to take 500,000 acres of public domain "would undoubtedly have been acceded to by Mexico if the Territory had remained hers," but Mexico had already recognized the Sonoita Grant. Thus the absurdity of the statement of the senate committee, with little knowledge of New Mexico, let alone of Mexico proper, becomes apparent.[32]

Another tract of land picked by the Baca heirs is the Valle Grande, six miles west of Los Alamos, the Baca Location No. 1. It is owned at this writing by the Dunigan family in Texas, which is negotiating with the U.S. Forest Service to sell it back to the government for up to $80 million. The senate bill which currently would provide authorization for the purchase, lists the following as reasons why the government should acquire the land: archaeological evidence of the use of the land will provide historical knowledge of territorial New Mexico; recreation; a model for sustainable land use; film sets remaining on the property that "are a significant part of the history of the American film industry"; and "so that the American people will not lose the opportunity presented by this resource to potential subdivisions."[33]

Reading between the lines, it become apparent that the Dunigan family, operating the land as the Baca Land and Cattle Company, have made a profit from the land somewhat beyond the traditional grazing and timber uses, by renting it to make Hollywood movies, and are now considering the possibility of subdividing the land. Little mention is made of the genesis of the Baca Location No. 1 or the possible land claims of neighboring pueblos.

The references that are made to the history of Baca Location No. 1 in U.S. Forest Service material, assessing the feasibility of purchase by the government and promoting such a purchase, contain major distortions and omissions. Most important is the lack of any comprehensive discussion of a federal policy regarding the management of government land that was once land-grant land.

Although the possible acquisition of Baca Location No. 1 has been studied intensively since 1990, there has been minimal public involvement in the process. The Forest Service has contacted some environmental groups and Indian pueblos, but land-grant organizations were not given an opportunity to express their opinions about a public land issue that originated as a land grant.[34] If the purchase of the Baca Location goes through, it appears that the use of the land will, not surprisingly, favor the concern of environmentalists. Yet when legislation is proposed to correct the injustices of land-grant adjudication under the Treaty of Guadalupe Hidalgo, objections are raised by the same environmentalists that local commons lands should not be made available to the land-grant communities that have traditionally used them.[35]

---

[32] For further discussion of the San José de Sonoita Grant see Richard W. Bradfute, *The Court of Private Land Claims: The Adjudication of Spanish and Mexican Land Grant Titles, 1891-1904* (Albuquerque: University of New Mexico Press, 1975), pp. 152-154.

[33] Senate Bill No. 1210, sponsored by Sen. Jeff Bingamon: "To authorize the acquisition of the Valle Caldera currently managed by the Baca Land and Cattle Company, and to provide for an effective management program for this resource within the Department of Agriculture, and consistent land management to protect the watershed of the Bandelier National Monument."

[34] *Report on the Study of the Baca Location No. 1* (U.S. Dept. of Agriculture, Santa Fe National Forest, n.d.), pp. 1-3, 51-54; videocassette, Baca Land Grant No. 1, Valle Grande, NM

[35] House of Representatives Bill No. 2538, sponsored by Rep. Bill Redmond: "To establish a Presidential commission to determine the validity of certain land claims arising out of the Treaty of Guadalupe-Hidalgo of 1848 involving the descendants of persons who were Mexican citizens at the time of the Treaty."

The change on the map before and after the treaty, in regard to the Baca Location, will be from green to red to green if this purchase goes through. But the green of the Mexican public domain is much different from the green of the U.S. Forest Service. First, it is costing the taxpayer millions of dollars to correct the government's mistake. More importantly, that huge sum of money will do nothing to correct the imbalance caused by the loss of common lands of community grants and other land loss caused by unfair land-grant decisions under the Treaty of Guadalupe Hidalgo. Scholars have pointed out recently that, when local commons become national commons such as Forest Service land, there is a concomitant loss of use-rights in traditional communities.[36]

VI. The Embudo Grant

An example of a valid grant that was unfairly rejected in its entirety is the Embudo Grant north of Santa Fé. Embudo had all requirements for validity under Spanish and Mexican law and practice, yet was rejected on a technicality. In 1725 Juan Márquez, Francisco Martín, and Lasaro de Córdova asked Governor Juan Domingo de Bustamante for a tract of land along the Embudo River that was later estimated to contain about 25,000 acres. Bounded by the Río Grande on the northwest and on the south by the Sebastián Martín Grant, the requested land overlapped land claimed by Picurís Pueblo, a situation that soon caused problems. Governor Bustamante approved the grant but, when the local *alcalde* tried to place the petitioners in possession of the land, he was met with a protest by the Picurís. The granted land encroached on Picurís private and common lands used by the pueblo for grazing and farming.[37]

At this early date soon after the Pueblo Revolt, the Spanish had not reached an accommodation with the Pueblo Indians concerning the amount of land to which a pueblo was entitled.[38] So the Picurís protest was dismissed when the Alcalde Vega y Coca determined that they had not farmed land within the Embudo Grant. The alcalde completed the act of possession by plucking up weeds and casting stones, and shouting "Long Live the King!" as the concrete symbols of ownership. The report of the act of possession completed the title papers, a copy of which was delivered to the grantees.[39]

The land was first settled by eight families who built homes around a central plaza with two watch towers (*torreones*) at the corners of the compound, to allow for warning of raids by Comanche or other Plains Indians. The settlement was abandoned due to such attacks, but was resettled soon by order of Governor Vélez Cachupin due to its importance as a buffer against Indian raids on Santa

---

[36] For an excellent study of how the once-common resource of game has lost its character as a resource of a local commons, see Louis Warren, *The Hunter's Game: Poachers and Conservationists in Twentieth Century America* (New Haven: Yale University Press, 1997).

[37] Petition of Juan Márquez, Francisco Martín, and Lasaro de Córdova to Gov. Bustamante, Río Arriba, NMLG-SG, file 91, Roll 31, fr. 285-286.

[38] Malcolm Ebright, "Advocates for the Oppressed: Indians, Genízaros and Their Spanish Advocates in New Mexico, 1700-1786," in *New Mexico Historical Review,* Vol. 71 (Oct. 1996), p. 305.

[39] Act of possession by Alcalde Miguel José de la Vega y Coca, Embudo, July 19, 1725. NMLG-SG, file 91, Roll 31, fr. 287-288.

Fe and other population centers. By the 1770s sixty-nine people were living on the grant and soon there were eight separate communities farming along the rivers that cut through the land.[40]

It is apparent from this brief early history of the Embudo Grant that it met the basic requirements for a valid land grant: documents evidencing the grant by the governor and settlement on the land. Yet the grant was rejected by the courts on a technicality. By the time the Embudo case finally came to trial in 1898, the government was looking for technicalities on which to base rejections. Millions of acres of questionable grants such as the Maxwell Grant and the Baca Locations had been confirmed as private grants, and public reaction to the fraud and land speculation embodied in the Santa Fé Ring had led to skepticism about land grants in general. The Court of Private Land Claims system did not allow for the easy ex-parte confirmations that had been pushed through congress by land speculators in the 1860s, because in the 1890s the lawyer for the government and his team of experts knew more about Hispanic law and practice than did the lawyers for land-grant claimants. Most important was the fact that no consistent body of law had been developed on the subject of Hispanic land-grant law. The laxness of the surveyors general in determining what was valid under Mexico was replaced by a strictness that often interpreted a Spanish or Mexican law in a way never dreamed of by those governments. That is exactly what happened with the Embudo Grant.[41]

By 1786 the original Embudo Grant documents in the hands of the grantees had become so worn that they requested their *alcalde* to make a certified copy of the grant. The alcalde, José Campo Redondo, laboriously copied every word of the grant documents and then signed a statement at the end indicating that the copy conformed to the original. It was this certified copy that was submitted to the Court of Private Land Claims. The U.S. attorney argued that the copy was invalid because it was not made by the proper official under Spanish law. If the copy was invalid, so was the grant, argued the government. The official authorized to make certified copies under the *Recopilación de leyes de los Reynos de las Indias* was called an *escríbano* (comparable to a U.S. notary), but none of these officials was to be found in Spanish or Mexican New Mexico during most of its history. Accordingly it was common for alcaldes to make certified copies of documents in New Mexico and to state that they were making the copy "for lack of a public or royal notary, there being none in this province."

This highly technical argument had been tried before and rejected, because the only way a grantee could have a copy made was to have an alcalde do it. Numerous certified copies of grant documents made by alcaldes had been submitted to the surveyor general and the Court of Private Land Claims and had been approved.[42]

The rejection of the Embudo Grant on the ground that the wrong official had made the certified copy of the grant papers, even though there was no doubt as to the existence of the Embudo Grant,

---

[40] Decree of Gov. Tomás Vélez Cachupin, Santa Fé, Feb. 21, 1750. Spanish Archives of New Mexico (SANM), I, No. 1100. Eleanor B. Adams and Fray Angélico Chávez, translators and annotators, *The Missions of New Mexico, 1776: A Description by Fray Francisco Atanasio Dominguez, with Other Contemporary Documents* (Albuquerque: University of New Mexico Press, 1956), p. 91.

[41] Ebright, *Land Grants,* pp. 37-51.

[42] Town of Bernalillo Grant, NMLG-PLC, Roll 52, case 208, fr. 21.

or the genuineness of the grant papers, shows how far the courts had come from the original intention of the Treaty of Guadalupe Hidalgo. Without a body of cases defining Mexican law and practice in New Mexico, the courts had free rein to come up with their own definitions. Remember the test of land-grant validity: to do as Mexico or Spain would have done. It would have been relatively easy in the Embudo situation to have examined what Spain and Mexico in fact did do regarding the Embudo Grant.

After the grant was made in 1725 it was temporarily abandoned because of Indian raids. Then it was one of several settlements that Governor Vélez Cachupin ordered resettled in 1750. His order and the fact of resettlement are strong indications of government recognition of the grant. The government wanted to keep Embudo viable as the first line of defense for Santa Fé and Santa Cruz de la Cañada. Unlike the Cabesa de Baca Grant, the same settlers who received the grant would resettle it, not a new group. The second aspect of Spanish recognition of the Embudo Grant was the making of a certified copy of the grant by alcalde Vega y Coca. As the local official with the most knowledge of land grants in the area, Vega y Coca could have refused to make the copy if he did not believe that the grant was valid. The third instance of Spanish recognition of the Embudo Grant occurred in 1795 when the neighboring Cieneguilla Grant was clearly an implied recognition of the Embudo Grant by the governor of New Mexico.[43]

Since these facts of recognition of the Embudo Grant were not urged upon the court, the Court of Private Land Claims rejected the grant. Even so, two justices registered a rare dissent from the majority opinion. Justices Joseph Reed and Wilbur Stone referred to the Treaty of Guadalupe Hidalgo on one hand and the decision of the majority of the court, on the other. The court's opinion, in the view of Reed and Stone, was requiring the Embudo claimants to meet the standard of proof required "in the establishment of a title of American origin," rather than looking at the Embudo Grant as the governments of Spain and Mexico would have done. The result, according to these dissenting justices, was that "the measures established by the government for the purpose of carrying out its treaty stipulations, would be made the instrument for defeating that purpose."[44]

This prophetic statement brings us down to the present where the question still remains, can the purpose and intent of the Treaty of Guadalupe Hidalgo still be fulfilled, at least partially, at this late date? The answer depends partly on what we as scholars do with the research that now enables us to analyze and understand these past events. We should not be afraid to make judgments as to the Mexican-American War of 1846-1848, the Treaty of Guadalupe Hidalgo and its solemn promises, and whether those promises have been fulfilled. In that regard, my view is similar to that of Nicholas Trist, who recalled his thoughts at the time of the signing: "[the treaty] was a thing for every right-minded American to be ashamed of."[45]

This shamefulness arises from the disparity in power between Mexico and the United States, which made the treaty "one of the harshest in modern history." The same imbalance was present

---

[43] Ebright, *Land Grants,* p. 134.
[44] NMLG-PLC, Roll 53, case 258, fr. 20.
[45] Ohrt, *Defiant Peacemaker,* pp. 145-146.

when the Baca Floats were awarded in the 1860s and when the Embudo decision was handed down in the 1890s. The advocates for privatization of the public domain were able to convince the senate committee to give them five choice tracts of land because no advocates for the communities using these lands were being heard at the time. The U.S. attorney was able to convince the Court of Private Land Claims to reject the Embudo Grant because the body of law interpreting the meaning of the Treaty of Guadalupe Hidalgo had reached an absurd hyper-technical construction that bore almost no relation to the law and practice of Spain and Mexico.

If there is room for optimism in this depressing picture, it is that the federal government either owns or is negotiating the purchase of the contested land involved in these two grants. The knowledge we now have about how the treaty's promises were broken regarding this land should be planted like a seed in our minds and in the minds of government officials now making decisions about this land. If we are serious about the importance of this history and of the land itself, we dare not let this seed die.

DEENA J. GONZALEZ

Dr. Deena J. González has perhaps a unique perspective on how life was and has been for the native inhabitants of the section of New Spain that became annexed to the United States under the Treaty of Guadalupe Hidalgo. Her specialization in the history of the indigenous folk of New Mexico is based on meticulous reserach methods, honed in the departments of history at New Mexico State University and the University of California, Berkeley, and now developed in her position on the faculty of Pomona College. The background for her profound insight is many generations of Spanish-speaking ancestors who learned to cope with the rarely benevolent conditions of life along the Río Grande.

Deena González was born into an educated family at the chile-producing center of Hatch, New Mexico. Her mother, for example, graduated from the University of New Mexico where she studied under Professor Lansing B. Bloom and others. Deena González's impressive academic career in administration, as well as in teaching and research, received an early boost with her selection for Phi Beta Kappa, election as President of the Graduate Assembly at Berkeley, and appointment to the National Research Council. She has been the chair of Chicano Studies at the Claremont Colleges; assistant coördinator at the Center of Latin American Studies at Berkeley; and co-chair of the Ford Foundation Fellows Conference in 1988-1989. Other professional responsibilities have included editorial work on such publications as *Aztlan* and *Signs;* proposal reviewing for such agencies as the American Council of Learned Societies and the National Endowment for the Humanities; and advisory positions such as board member of the Women of the West Museum in Denver, Colorado, and mentor for the Program in Collegiate Scholars in History at the University of Florida.

Increasingly, since the publication of her dissertation, "The Spanish-Mexican Women of Santa Fé: Patterns of Their Resistance and Accommodation, 1820-1880," Dr. González's work has focused on the Hispanic women of the American Southwest. In deference to the two strains of the culture, she uses the precise term, "Spanish-Mexican," to indicate that the indigenous people of the area are genetically, for the most part, the descendants of a variety of Indian tribesmen with some admixture of European blood. Upon this ancient heritage of emigration, ultimately from the Orient, has been grafted in the last half-millenium the European culture of the Spanish invaders, particularly their Romance language and Catholicism. In contrast, the more popular term, "Hispanic," denotes only Spanish-speaking, with no indication of genetic origin or other cultural factors. The term "Latina" is even broader since it denotes a person who may not even speak Spanish. Although her fluent and idiomatic Spanish continues to be invaluable in her research, González observes somewhat ruefully,

"Control of language—in this case, still, English—assists mobility, geographic, sexual, and economic."

Dr. González has studied the lives of ordinary women, especially the single ones—widows, abandoned wives, unmarried females—who lost the only status that their society accorded them when they found themselves without husbands. She has analyzed the effects of class, racial identity, and wealth on the legal judgments involving women in the borderlands. She has investigated the operation of legend in the stories of two most untypical women: the 19th-century entrepreneur of Santa Fé, Doña Gertrudis Barceló, and the colonial-period linguist, Malintzin Tenepal ("Malinche"). She has brought the discourse on the position of Spanish-Mexican women in our society up to date with comments on tensions now encountered in the workplace, especially in academia, where women of the category are still notably under-represented. In this context, she has written about the hostility that many Hispanic men display against Hispanic women who occupy professional positions; they lag in the acceptance of their ethnic counterparts who are working outside of traditional domestic occupations. Of particular concern to such men, whose personal identity is often rooted in their gender, are those women who regard themselves as homosexual.

Before she began her investigation of the effects of the change of government upon New Mexico's native population in the 19th century, Dr. González was already familiar with the conditions of their lives. In "The Spanish Borderlands" she examines the sexual hierarchy, the class system, and the penalties applied to women who did not conform to the rigid mores of colonial society. In "The Widowed Women of Santa Fé: Assessments of the Lives of an Unmarried Population, 1850-1880," she gleans much information from the registered wills that women prepared to distribute their usually meager belongings—and extrapolates the lack of improvement in their financial condition after the arrival of General Stephen W. Kearny. Though business boomed under "gringo" enterprise, wages for natives did not increase. For women the old occupations of laundress and cook left them less able to contend with inflated prices than before. The focus on one woman who was able to take advantage of the changed conditions under the new régime is in "La Tules of Image and Reality: Euro-American Attitudes and Legend Formation on a Spanish-Mexican Frontier." The examination of legend vs. fact in the story of this remarkable saloon keeper reveals much about the attitudes that shaped the lives of all citizens in the new American borderland territories.

Frances Hernández
University of Texas at El Paso

ON THE LIVES OF WOMEN AND CHILDREN

IN THE AFTERMATH OF

THE UNITED STATES-MEXICAN WAR

Deena J. González

Recently, in the field of history, social historians especially have begun to unpack the larger meanings of such tired and true topics as frontier history, pioneer women, western history and ethnohistory. Many have contributed to this effort, not to debunk but to place into the world of history different notions about how people lived in the last century, about what they valued, whom they admired, and what place or space they occupied. Moving away from the notion that history is a science, that it can be unbiased or objective, historians these past forty or so years have unraveled many topics, including that of women and children, to arrive at conclusions we might not have thought possible in our lifetime. The impact of the United States-Mexican War is one such topic.

Until recent decades, and before important books revealed what Mexicans themselves thought about this war, it was common to assume that Mexico caused its own demise, that it lost land and people because it was bankrupt, needy, and could not control its own borders. In book after book, historians began to revise this assessment, saying that an aggressive U.S. foreign policy, a well worked-out territorial imperative, coupled with some savvy Euro-American merchants and traders, designed to take possession of Mexico's far north. Historians like David J. Weber in the 1970s would add to this debate by suggesting or recommending that the former Mexican north, this place we reside in today, is a colonized land where native and Mexican residents were displaced a hundred years ago, slowly, gradually. The statistics for northern New Mexico prove the point: by all estimates, twenty years after the war, nearly ninety percent of land and property formerly in the hands of the Spanish-Mexican residents was in the hands of the enterprising Euro-Americans.[1]

What of the women and children? Were they or are we simply to look at them as impoverished, grief-stricken, shy, grin-and-bear-its? Or may we not view them as active agents, actresses cast upon this magnificent cultural and political stage? I think we can say, and I offer you this message: the

---

[1] See David J. Weber, ed., *New Spain's Far Northern Frontier: Essays on Spain in the American West, 1540-1821* (Albuquerque: University of New Mexico Press, 1979), and Malcolm Ebright, *Land Grants and Lawsuits in Northern New Mexico* (Albuquerque: University of New Mexico Press, 1994), Still useful are Roxanne Dunbar Ortiz, *Roots of Resistance: Land Tenure in New Mexico, 1680-1980* (Los Angeles: Chicano Studies Research Center, 1980), and Victor Westphall, *Mercedes Reales: Hispanic Land Grants of the Upper Rio Grande Region* (Albuquerque: University of New Mexico Press, 1983).

women of the borderlands did indeed live through war and later grim reminders of war, and they did more than merely bear it. The children of the time similarly appear to have continued many of the traditions of their parents. At least the documents rarely refer to problem children or delinquencies; shame could explain it, but probably hard work, poverty, and subsistence living go further in characterizing the role of children in Mexican society, especially after the war. Survival, though, we in Chicano/a Studies like to say, is not history; survivors typically tell stories of resistance and of affirmation but they usually do so with the balance of some horrible event in their backgrounds. This, too, is the case for the Spanish-Mexican, Hispano, Mexican people of New Mexico after the United States settled its differences with Mexico.

Stories help shape our perceptions of life in this area of the country after the earliest Euro-American immigration, which began in the 1820s and peaked in the 1870s. In those sixty years, many historians say, three cultures harmoniously came together, the Euro-American, Spanish-Mexican, and Native American. "Tricultural harmony" makes for a terrific motto but in the 1800s, as today, cultural interaction was actually noisy, upsetting and rather disharmonious. I offer three examples involving social interactions, the courtroom as the setting, and the outcome revealing something of the cultural and political climate after the war.

The widow Chaves was wealthy and determined to write her will in 1871. Unable to read or write English, she turned to a law clerk, Edwin Dunn, to draw up the document. He seemed interested in helping her. To her horror, she would later tell a friend, her son discovered when he returned from a trip that the clerk and an unscrupulous priest had colluded, and in her will were giving the church and the poor a large sum of her money. This upper-class woman claimed to have been spared embarrassment, by her son's discovery, and subsequently asked her neighbor, the widow Delgado, to witness the burning of this despised document.[2]

What strikes me as interesting about this case is the feature of a conspiring law clerk and a priest, reported on by another outsider to Santa Fé, Territorial Secretary William G. Ritch. In his recollection of this story, as it had been told to him, Ritch highlighted what he wanted people to remember, that a lawyer (clerk) and a Catholic priest were equally culpable of duping ordinary citizens, in this case a widow. The retelling of this story through his eyes and from his perspective suited his purpose well, that Spanish-Mexicans were a "priest-ridden" citizenry.

But what of the widow Chaves? Can we not say more about her design and intention? These are, after all, things historians can barely begin to describe. The documents tell a wonderful story. In this case, I searched until I found a will I believe to have belonged to the same widow Chaves. It is long, by the standards of her time, over twelve pages, and it defines her upper-class status. The document describes her poor health, followed by a long prayer, then a long list of properties and farm equipment, sheep and pastures, houses and furniture follows her rich Catholic expression of prayer. The inventory attests to her power through longevity, of her crisis management, and of parent-child relations. The widow Chaves ordered her heirs to pay for masses for her, to distribute

---

[2] The widow's first name was not cited in the MS Official Reports of the Territorial Secretary, Summer 1876, Ritch Collection, RI 1731, Henry E. Huntington Library, San Marino, CA.

among themselves her worldly possessions, and to care for servants and for shepherds working under her as well.[3]

Given the length and precision of the inventory, one question becomes, when all is said and done, was the widow duped or was she doing her own share of testing these new and muddy waters presented by a new Euro-American system of governance, of a separation of church and state, required by that system in legal and educational matters? In other words, did she provide her own escape clause by asking (and knowing) her son would catch the mistake and help entrap the law clerk and French priest putting their hands on her money? They could hardly deny having perpetrated the deed, and one can nearly hear the territorial authority—whose role was indeed to ensure the separation of church and state as the U.S. government required—chortling when he reported that the widow Chaves no longer had the same faith in the priesthood she once had. Another question, though, is which priesthood, the local one or the imported French priesthood?

Poor women in the decades after the war faced other travails. Looking at adoption petitions and cases, I have found several examples of how differences, cultural and social, made themselves known. Ana Marta Carson was called before a judge to explain why he should not award custody of her four-year-old daughter to Henry Carson, the child's father, a Euro-American. Ana Marta pleaded poverty when asked why she had abandoned the child, leaving her with Henry and his new wife. In another instance, Florence Donaghue petitioned to adopt his[sic] infant daughter because the mother, Antonia Gallegos, was "quite poor and unable to support and properly care for said child." He won custody but, interestingly, Antonia Gallegos appears later in an inventory of his estate as Antonia Gallegos de Donaghue, so that story might have had a happy ending.[4]

In a third case, the widow Tomasa Fitzmaurice had to answer a judge's call repeatedly about her husband's will, its authenticity, and her marriage to the Euro-American. "I have always lived in Santa Fé," she responded when asked about her residence. Fed up, Fitzmaurice in the same period filed another will, her own, at the church in the presence of witnesses, saying she did not "understand these foreigners [who] are so preoccupied with affairs that are my own, with our business and customs." If we listen closely to this language, we can almost hear the clashing of cultures and values in the background.

Until recently, calling attention to this sort of tension was considered unwise among historians. Yet we always have known that it existed and that, in many instances, women formed networks of power and authority in politics and in the economy. In other work and in my book, I spend many pages detailing stories and legends about the most famous woman this side of the Mississippi, Doña Gertrudes Barceló, La Tules of Santa Fé gambling saloon fame and fortune. Born in 1800 and dead in 1852, La Tules encompasses this pre-U.S.-Mexican War period. Her death followed only one year after Bishop Jean Baptiste Lamy was sent to these hinterlands to fix up the Catholic Church. In her fifty-two years this "infamous" figure and gambling authority witnessed many changes, indeed

---

[3] See María (de la) Nieves Chavez, Santa Fe County Records, MS Book D, Dec. 1870-Jan. 1871, pp. 27-66.

[4] See Santa Fe County Records, MS Legitimacy and Adoption Record, 1870-1882, pp. 3-4, 7-8. On Gallego's marriage to Donaghue, see Santa Fe County Records, MS Probate Court Journal, 1877-1897, Inventory of Florence Donaghue, Book E, p. 510.

argued on their behalf. With funds from American soldiers who descended on Santa Fé, as well as from subsequent groups of travelers and authorities, she maintained a bank account that was large by any measure. When the government could not meet its payroll, it is said she bankrolled it.[5]

At her saloon travelers new to Santa Fé and older, seasoned residents, men and women alike, learned a new language. The card games required very little linguistic facility in either Spanish or English. Story after story have highlighted how this one woman relieved the lonely soldiers of two things—their boredom and their cash. Today I write about Barceló, I study the meaning of her life, because while such a re-reading of her times is necessary, in her own time she was disparaged and her culture suffered degradation in the public domain. Describing women's dresses of her time, George Kendall called them "indelicate" and "immodest." Matt Field reported that her "loose dress" was designed as an affect, "seeming to study negligence." Josiah Gregg stipulated that La Tules had risen from poverty, was a woman of "shady character" and "a common prostitute ... a whore and a gambler."

Of her male relatives or the men in her community, others, like James Josiah Webb, twenty years a merchant in Santa Fé, would say that in the entire town, "the Pinos and Ortizes were considered the 'ricos' and those most respectable leaders in society and political influence, but idleness, gambling, and the Indians had made such inroads upon their influence that there was little left except the reputation of honorable descent." George Kendall called the Spanish-Mexicans of New Mexicans "an anti-go-ahead race." The descriptors are hardly surprising: William Becknell, credited with initiating the Santa Fé trade, said, "The people are generally swarthy, and live in a state of extreme indolence and ignorance." The buildings, the architecture, was described as low, squat and dark, with nothing present, Webb reported, that would induce him to "entertain a desire to become a resident." He and others described Santa Fé as a "parcel of brick yards," its streets "narrow and filthy," the walkways littered with "monte banks" and "beggarly people," the residents "treacherous" and "proverbial liars," who have "three or four prices for everything sold." Historians might well offer the lesson here about how things change, for today that same parcel of bricks is worth a very strong U.S. dollar![6]

The presence of these newcomers and especially of their dollars did indeed change the tenor of life in Santa Fé and all along the Santa Fé-Chihuahua Trail. To the north, especially, the sojourner became far more well known than before, the person heading to the gold fields. To the south, the

---

[5] On La Tules and citations for Euro-American immigrants to Santa Fé, 1820-1846, consult articles by me including: "La Tules of Image and Reality," in Adela de la Torre & Beatriz M. Pesquera, eds. *Building with Our Hands: New Directions in Chicana Studies* (Berkeley: University of California Press, 1993) and also in Vicki L. Ruiz & Ellen C. DuBois, eds., *Unequal Sisters: A Multicultural Reader in U.S. Women's History* (2d ed. New York: Routledge, 1994); "From La Leyenda Negra to La Tules," in J. Phillip Langellier, ed., *The Mask of Zorro: Mexican Americans in Popular Media* (Los Angeles: Gene Autrey Museum, 1994); and "The Widowed Women of Santa Fe: Assessments on the Lives of an Unmarried Population, 1850-1880," in Arlene Scadron, ed., *On Their Own: Widows and Widowhood in the American Southwest, 1848-1939* (Urbana: University of Illinois Press, 1988) and also in Ruiz and DuBois, eds., *Unequal Sisters.*

[6] For the quotation from James Josiah Webb see his MS memoirs, 1844-1889, History Library Museum of New Mexico, Santa Fé: on Kendall see Milo M. Quaife, ed., *Narrative of the Texan Santa Fe Expedition*, by George Wilkins Kendall (Chicago: R.R. Donnelley, 1929). See also John E. Sunder, ed., *Matt Field on the Santa Fe Trail* (Norman: University of Oklahoma Press, 1960), p. 222; and *The Personal Narrative of James O. Pattie*, intro. by William Goetzmann (Philadelphia: Lippincott, 1962).

merchants and the lawyers who followed on their heels altered more than just the highways. These men occasionally married Spanish-Mexican, sometimes Native American, women and they sometimes abandoned them as well.

In January 1847, resisters to the Euro-American takeover caught and scalped Governor Charles Bent, or so the story goes, leaving him to die. The murder of an army lieutenant who had been pursuing horse thieves occurred in the spring. Forty-three Spanish-Mexicans were brought to Santa Fé to stand trial for the crime—a bit of exaggeration given that only one bullet killed him. Lieutenant Alexander Dyer, writing in his journal, reported on "a large meeting of citizens at the Palace," where speakers expressed much dissatisfaction. Shortly after, he would write that reports were filtering in that the "Mexicans are to rise and attack us." Such conditions, all the way up to the signing of the Treaty of Guadalupe Hidalgo, could hardly be called harmonious or be viewed as matters of adjustment or of reaching an accord.[7]

The consequences of political turmoil and economic hardship spelled disaster for women and children. As I have documented elsewhere, women's wages declined in this period and, more than ever before, they were forced to take on several wage-earning jobs at once as laundress, seamstress and domestic. With falling wages, my research has shown that the size of ordinary households grew in the case of Santa Fé, and I surmise this was so in Las Cruces and Albuquerque as well. More people lived under one roof, with wages as well as an internal economy of chicken raising, sheepherding, and so on, supporting larger numbers of people. The demographics of these times suggests subsistence, perseverance, and very little wealth or accumulated assets, except within a tiny proportion of the population.

How did women cope? Sister Blandina Segale in the 1840s, surveying the problems in Santa Fé, documented the costs of ordinary items such as eggs, meat, and simple tools such as hoes or sickles. Their prices rose steadily. The need for day laborers to clear away fields, to cultivate them and to build stores signaled a change overall.[8] The remedy for women and children lay in wage labor. Children accompanied women regularly, in domestic service or in work conducted outside the home, like laundering and food preparation. Santa Fé's slow pace belied the bustle of a new economy just beneath the surface. Writing letters in the 1870s, Mrs. Henry Wetter would describe the "tawdry" Catholic processions she witnessed, with "dolls" dressed up in fine cloth and paraded through the streets. (She meant Catholic processions of saints.) She also described the constant pounding and hammering of building going on all around her. In other words, the noise and dust and busy tempo continued from the time just before the treaty was signed until the 1870s, some thirty years later.[9]

Coping and surviving are two accurate words for the conditions of life for Spanish-Mexican women. I have recently begun to focus also on the air of resignation that permeated cultural and social life in the decades following the Treaty of Guadalupe Hidalgo. The picture in this regard is clearly skewed by the sorts of document I have been able to collect in a project of translation

---

[7] Alexander M. Dyer, "Mexican War Journal, 1846-1848," MS copy, History Library, Museum of New Mexico, Santa Fe, pp. 96, 97.

[8] [Sister] Blandina Segale, *At the End of the Santa Fe Trail* (Milwaukee: Bruce Publishing Co., 1948), p. 104.

[9] Mrs. Henry Wetter, MS letter to her sister, April 3, 1877, History Library, Museum of New Mexico, Santa Fe.

and transcription: over forty wills written by Spanish-Mexican women in the period we are considering here, chosen only by virtue of their legibility and from a number of sources such as probate court journals, private papers, and miscellaneous records in the court system.

Wills, I should say, generally offer a final reprieve or resolution; that is not unusual. Their tone as well as the specific acts of conveyance—the way they give property away—detail areas of concern and demonstrate faith, Catholic faith, which of course then as now preaches to some extent acceptance, devotion and filial duty. To what extent the following stories show some combination of all of the above, the reader must decide. Your comments on these are invited.

I have usually not attempted to study avid or active Catholicism in my work as it seems to present many more problems than solutions for historians. Why people of this age believed what they did is something about which we can only guess or surmise. How they sustained their devotion to the cult of saints and to the practice of rituals and community embedded in Catholic theology is more subject to guessing than to good theorizing, because few of them wrote explicitly about their views on the church, god, or saints.

In prayerful meditations and in lament-filled comments embedded in their final wishes, the forty documents stand as a testament to women's voice and authority. We can only suppose how often their wishes were followed. I can discern that in the 1870s women began leaving their sons property, lands, pastures and houses, more often than their daughters. This is a distinct departure from practice before the war when many left most of their estates to daughters. This does not apply to any particular class, from the wealthiest to the poorest. Women deposited their last testaments at the church and in court.

The wealthier women, such as María Nieves Chaves (the widow of Secretary Ritch's story above?), bequeathed estates such as hers: 4 rooms in La Ciénega, 420 feet of land located in Los Palacios (varas), another amount of land in the same place, 560 feet of land, another 450 varas of land, altogether 4 parcels she estimated to be worth more than $100. Household articles included 3 mattresses, 3 blankets, 2 straw mattresses, 4 pillows, 5 large santos, 6 small santos, 11 salt cellars, 1 small cigar case, a wooden table, 3 wooden stools, 35 sacks of corn, some wool, about 3.2 bushels of corn flour, wooden boxes, 3 china plates, 4 china cups, 1 china tray, 6 vases, 1 flat iron for cooking, 1 iron pot, a wooden bucket, a grinding stone, a small cast iron pot, 2 axes, 1 sieve, 1 rifle, firewood, a metal tire, 4 plows, 1 rug with a leaf design, 1 underground room (a root cellar), 4 pairs of shearing tools, 4 large donkeys and 1 small donkey, 2 large oxen, 7 pairs of oxen, three years old, 1 four-year-old bull, 1 three-year-old ox, 4 two-year-old calves, 4 three-year-old calves, 12 pregnant cows, 60 big sheep, 43 small lambs, 6 goats, 41 big goats, 1 pig, and 1 horse and horse saddle. Debts owed to her included goats, sheep, corn and wheat, plus the labor of several shepherds. The value of these worldly possessions, by the probate officer's estimation based on this will, amounted to $1447. Included in the final copy of the settled estate, that is, after her death, were charges of $35 for a coffin and $40 to the priest, P.A. Truchard. Death was costly.[10]

---

[10] Will of María (de la) Nieves Chavez, pp. 27-66.

Desideria Otero submitted her final wishes in the same year. The contrasts between these two documents highlight what might allow us to call Chaves upper class and Otero not. Otero began:

> encomiendo mi alma a mi Dios y criador de ella al cual humildemente suplico que cuando fuere su santisima voluntad de sacar a mi alma y desatarla de las cadenas de este corritible cuerpo my alma encomiendo a Dios que la crio y redimio y mi cuerpo mando a la tierra de donde fue formado mando mi entierro sea umilde y en la forma de aransel en uno de los seminterios, mis santos abogados el santo de mi nombre y San Francisco de Asis y mi Senor de Guadalupe y el Santo Angel de mi guarda ... .[11]

She continues that she was "married and cared for by" (*casada y belada con el finado*) Pablo Quintana, for thirty years, and they had three children, now dead. She begins to itemize: 2 small rooms "I leave to be sold so that I might be buried." She declares as well a burro, 6 mattresses, 2 coverlets, one of wool, 1 saint to go to her comadre Ventura, another 9; 11 mirrors, 7 pillows, 1 tunic, 1 cover, 2 sheets; to Lupita Quintana she leaves 2 skirts with a slip, 1 pair of eyeglasses, 1 glass, 3 plates of china, 3 cups, 2 spoons; all of the other items are to be distributed among two heirs, both men, one whose last name matches that of the two male witnesses — relatives we may presume.[12]

Between the wealthy María Nieves Chaves and the more impoverished Desideria Otero was a gap whose significance we might contemplate. The more interesting thing, however, is the other gap, the one separating women like Chaves, perhaps with equally wealthy Spanish-Mexican men (by my estimation, not even 5% of the population of Santa Fé) from the majority of those 200-plus Euro-American men who by 1870 had begun to control local politics and the economy. By all measures, Chaves's inventory and net worth suggest that she is more comparable to the white day laborers who were entering the town, some still on their way to California, but others there to work the mines or ranches that were springing up throughout the 1870s.[13]

As the railroad in that decade approached their town, the women and children of Santa Fé and environs watched with some dismay as their buying ability plummeted. Their lives now were determined by wages more than ever. This shift to a wage economy was the single most drastic impact upon New Mexico's population of the resolution of conflict the Treaty of Guadalupe Hidalgo symbolized.

To the present day, most international conflicts are the result of two giants or political entities, one from the north and the other from the south, each flexing their muscles as it were. These sorts of male metaphors or body-building images are perfectly appropriate here. The nineteenth was indeed

---

[11] I trust my soul in God its creator from whom I humbly seek at the moment when he calls for it, and breaks the chain binding my worldly body to return to be with he who created it. I redeem my body to the earth from which it was formed. She asks that her saints be distributed, saint of my name, saints who watch over me ... . Will of Desideria Otero, Santa Fe County Records, MS Book D, Dec. 1870, pp. 30-31.

[12] *Ibid.*, p. 31.

[13] For details on the role of inflation, declining wages, and comparisons, see Table 3 in my "Widowed Women of Santa Fe."

a masculine century, dominated by wars and empire-building, by threats and invasions, by truces and settlements. The United States had invaded Mexico and stripped her of half of her lands. But what was at play inside the very same territories, now folded into the United States by virtue of a treaty and not by the vote of any local population, was an agreement among the Desideria Oteros and the María Chaveses that life was different. Few people then or today would bother asking what did the Spanish-speaking, Catholic residents of the Mexican north feel about the United States takeover. Even fewer would try to ascertain exactly what these women or children thought about shifting political loyalties or about a changed economy that moved from subsistence to wages, that was shaped by such industrial features as the railroad and external markets, and all that these implied.

Let us also try to think through the implications not simply of oversight or neglect, crucial though those issues are in women's and family history, but also what it means to focus on great national questions and not on the impact of the nation-state on its people. Mexico was indeed broke, its treasury in some disrepair, and the United States had survived and would survive in the 1870s a financial crisis in the silver market. Those two nations and their political systems both had tremendous potential. This was indeed the century when each, in its march toward industrialization, would come face to face with poverty, that most vexing problem of modern industrialization. Mexico's embarrassment over losing not just territory but its people, Spanish and indigenous, still lingers. The Treaty of Guadalupe Hidalgo guaranteed rights of property, respect for religion and educational values, and land rights. Alas, these pledges would be broken repeatedly over the decades during and after the war. In Santa Fé, the list of lawyers who followed boundary commissioners and land commissions seemed endless, led by Thomas B. Catron's inner circle and Land Commissioner William Pelham; even the census taker was a friend of the big lawyers and speculators. The presence of poor women and children meant to many of these men that a population ripe for exploitation was available, and exploit it they did. How? They employed women as laundresses, seamstresses and domestics. Ninety percent of all adult women worked for substandard wages in these jobs between 1850 and 1880. In court case after court case, Euro-American men acquired houses and pastures, sometimes for a pittance—$1.25 in one instance from a man named Valencia who had failed to file the proper papers with the land commission.[14]

If women then were surviving as laborers, is there anything else we can say about them to cast this situation of destitution or of declining status in a more positive light? That is certainly an impulse historians have. I can say that leaving readers and audiences with a true portrayal of harsh reality, of ethnic tensions and conflicts, is too much reality in a single dose. We have all grown up with this cloud of the nation-state looming over us, in one form or another. Take the old saw, "In 1492 Columbus sailed the ocean blue ..." and move on to subsequent questionings and grumblings about the meaning of Columbus or, in the case of Mexico, Cortés. We know that families and women and children survived these most trying times of the 19th century and, grim though the reminders of life then are, it would be a mistake to suggest that its inheritance was mostly positive rather than

---

[14] See Howard Roberts Lamar, *The Far Southwest, 1846-1912: A Territorial History* (New York: Norton, 1970), pp. 138, 140-141.

negative on people in this part of the world. Yes, cultural traditions thrived and much remains in Spanish Catholicism of which we can be proud. Significantly, it is these untold stories of some terror, fear, and decline that humanize the period for us. Picture Desideria Otero and her small group of witnesses, gathered to parcel out a tiny number of worldly possessions—but in that single act, linking the mundane with the profane and the spiritual. Similarly we need, I suggest through examples and stories of these women's lives, to link past and present, remembering the 19th-century travails of our *antepasados*.

JOSEFINA ZORAIDA VAZQUEZ

Suppose for a moment that a planning committee holding a conference on the Treaty of Guadalupe Hidalgo was given carte blanche in selecting a scholar to present Mexico's viewpoint. And the planning committee's only requirement was that the person picked must be the finest diplomatic historian in Mexico.

That fits rather precisely Dr. Josefina Zoraida Vázquez. Her credentials speak for themselves. Her degrees are as follows: M.A. from the Universidad Nacional Autónoma de México (UNAM); not one but two Ph.D's—one from the Universidad Central de Madrid (Spain) and a second from UNAM. In addition she had a postdoctoral appointment at Harvard University.

But it is in the arena of her publications that her qualifications are not only outstanding but also unique. She is an extraordinarily prolific historian, having authored or co-authored some twenty-five monographs including most recently *La intervención Norteamericana, 1846-1848,* published in 1997 by the Secretaría de Relaciones Exteriores, Mexico City. In addition she has edited or co-authored another twenty-one books on Mexican history. Furthermore, she has written chapters in an equal number of edited volumes in Mexican history, and as many or more articles in a variety of distinguished academic journals including *Historia Mexicana.*

In addition to her phenomenal publication record, Dr. Vázquez has had a distinguished teaching career at UNAM and El Colegio de México, where she is currently a research professor; also at the University of Texas at Austin (as a visiting professor and as Tinker Professor), the University of Puerto Rico as visiting professor, McWane Visiting Professor at Duke University, and visiting professor at the University of Florence (Italy) and the University of California, Berkeley.

In the arena of fellowships and awards, Dr. Vázquez takes a back seat to no one. She was a recipient of an Organization of American States (OAS) Fellowship; a Rockefeller Foundation Fellowship; a Farmer Fellowship; a Tinker Professorship; a Fulbright Foundation Distinguished Lecturer; an Ida Beam Distinguished Lecturer at the University of Iowa; a Guggenheim Fellowship; a Fulbright Fellowship; OAS Andrés Bello Prize; and she has been a Fellow of the Center for Advanced Studies in the Behavioral Sciences at Stanford University. In the area of scholarship, she has served as editor of Mexico's leading historical journal, *Historia Mexicana;* and as a member of the editorial boards of the *Hispanic American Historical Review* and of the *Journal of World History.*

Finally, among her administrative chores, she has chaired the Centro de Estudios Históricos of el Colegio de México for some six years.

One is hard pressed to suggest a more distinguished scholar to define in a historical and diplomatic sense the position of the Mexican government and its people on the origins and impact of the Treaty of Guadalupe Hidalgo to the present day.

Professor Louis R. Sadler
New Mexico State University

THE SIGNIFICANCE IN MEXICAN HISTORY

OF THE TREATY OF GUADALUPE HIDALGO

Josefina Zoraida Vázquez

The conduct of the government of the United States, in the affairs relating to Texas, has been an uninterrupted series of aggressions against us. Having failed in obtaining the objects of its constant attacks, this government has affronted the world by presenting itself as the aggrieved one while, after having violated our territory, it has spilled the blood of our compatriots over it.

Manuel Crecencio Rejón

For the Mexican people, the war with the United States and its corollary, the Treaty of Guadalupe Hidalgo, have left a very bitter memory. In the United States the war has been almost forgotten and does not merit more than a few pages in university textbooks, in spite of its having given to the nation the territory which made it a continental power; and the treaty is remembered only in a part of the southwest. Of course, it must be stated that there is a fundamental difference which explains different approaches to history in the two countries: while almost all Mexicans share an identical past, most North Americans do not, because what happened longer ago than a half century is totally unknown to them.

In its own time, the war also produced different reactions. In the United States it provoked the excitement described by Professor Robert Johannsen in his book, *To the Halls of the Montezumas; The Mexican War in the American Imagination,*[1] sufficient to challenge all of the most eager moralists. Mexicans, on the other hand, were overcome by a profound, collective depression. Thus Carlos María de Bustamante, witness to the occupation of Mexico City, wrote in his *Diario* on the 15th of September, 1847: "The Mexican Republic is finished, its independence and liberty ended by foolishly imitating the institutions of the country by which it has been enslaved." His words remind us that from the time of independence the United States had been the model for the neighboring nation which, as he believed, had led Mexico to disaster.

The signing of the Treaty of Guadalupe Hidalgo was rejected by many Mexicans, even though a large part of the country was occupied, her seaports blockaded, and the lands of the present southwestern United States conquered and brazenly annexed; they wanted to fight "to the last man."

---

[1] New York: Oxford University Press, 1985.

Manuel Crecencio Rejón in his "Observaciones sobre el Tratado de Guadalupe *[sic]*," commented that, if the document were signed,

> We are not only supposed to remain silent while our unjust neighbors make off with the lands which they had at first selected for themselves, but we must also pay them for earning and taking them and others as well, and finally we are expected to confess that they had the right to all this.[2]

He predicted the loss of nationality in some ten or fifteen years, fears encouraged, surely, by the movement to annex all of Mexico which the military victories had inspired in a goodly number of North Americans. This disappointment converted some expansionists into filibusters who operated along the border for more than a decade. In truth it is surprising that Mexico did not lose more territory than that of Mesilla in 1853, since the greed of the North American presidents during the 1850s was also insatiable, and they wanted at least Baja California, Sonora and all of the northern Mexican states. In spite of this menace, with the exception of the "cession" forced at Mesilla, which disgracefully was the fertile land where New Mexicans had moved who wanted to continue to be Mexicans, the boundary has been modified only by the capriciousness of the Río Bravo [Río Grande]. Thus, history has seemed to justify the moderates who had accepted the sad, but inevitable fate in negotiating the Treaty of Guadalupe Hidalgo. Don Manuel de la Peña y Peña, provisional president in those black days, insisted in his speech before the Mexican congress on May 7, 1848, that

> The cession of territory was the least that could be agreed upon and that it was not possible to hope that in this matter, the United States would modify its demands. As large as are the territories of Texas, Upper California, and New Mexico, the government of the United States has declared to its Congress that without the cession of these territories it will continue the war under the plan as indicated by the president in his message of the sixth of December of last year. Given the desirability of a peace settlement, the negotiations cannot be condemned for not having lessened the loss of territory, and perhaps they even deserve praise for having seen to it that the first territorial demands were not later increased—especially in view of the facts that the capital was lost and the army, which evacuated it on the thirteenth of September, was disbanded.[3]

Nevertheless, Rejón was correct to argue that the acceptance of an indemnity would be interpreted as a sale of territory, and would impede recovery from the enormous damages inflicted upon us. The idea that the $15 million was payment for territory has prevailed, in spite of its absurdity, as Rejón himself said that, if "more than eighty-one thousand square miles" were sold for that amount, it would appear that all of Mexico's territory would be worth approximately 450 to 500 million pesos. Furthermore in periodicals, books and even maps the territory continues to be mentioned as

---

[2] Manuel Crecencio Rejón, "Observation on the Treaty of Guadalupe," in Cecil R. Robinson, ed., *The View from Chapultepec* (Tucson: University of Arizona Press, 1989), pp. 95-96.

[3] Manuel de la Peña y Peña, "An Address in Support of the Treaty of Guadalupe. Delivered to the Mexican Congress on May 7, 1848," in Robinson, *View,* pp. 106-107.

purchased from Mexico, as in the cases of Louisiana and Alaska. Robert Sainz Holguín in the *El Paso Times* of February 2, this year, points out that "Mexico was paid $15,000,000 for its territories," and René Romo in the *Albuquerque Journal* of February 1 affirms, "As a result of the treaty, the United States took possession of the Southwestern territories in return for a $15 million payment."

Mexicans still scarcely have a definite idea about what their contemporaries wanted to make very clear. Manuel de la Peña y Peña in his cited writing insisted:

> The territories ceded by the treaty have not been given up for the sum of fifteen million dollars, but to recover our ports and invaded cities, to put a definite stop to all types of evils and horrors, to console the multitude of families who have abandoned their homes and trades and are reduced or in process of being reduced to beggary.

The Mexican commissioners who negotiated the treaty were careful to explain their true feeling precisely:

> Regarding the indemnification that was agreed to in the twelfth and following articles, some explanations are needed. We would insult common sense if we failed to show that this indemnification was not a payment for the people of the ceded lands, because no person of sober judgment could think (especially after seeing Articles VIII and IX) that the Mexican government had intended to sell, and that the United States had intended to buy people ... . But we must protest that the cited indemnification was scarcely adequate in view of the territory that remained for the successful continuation of our existence. The lost lands had not been sold under the treaty; they had been lost in the war; the war had determined, by the sword, the boundary between the United States and Mexico ... . It was the greatest amount that we could obtain as compensation for the damages that the Republic suffered. It [the Republic] was reduced by the amount of land that her neighbor acquired, in spite of the now reduced population and the smaller nation, which bore the same obligations as before, [which were] consequently still more burdensome. Thus our domestic and foreign obligations remained to be borne entirely by the part of the Mexican nation that retained that name, while without the cession the burden would have been distributed over the whole republic as it had previously existed. Damages of this kind may be repaired in part by means of indemnification.[4] [See Appendix on page 93 for the original Spanish.]

The loss of territory was the more bitter because of the fact that it was an unjust war, without any basis except for territorial expansion. As John S.D. Eisenhower states in his book, *So Far from God; the U.S. War with Mexico,* "the fact is that Mexico stood in the way of the American Dream of Manifest Destiny."[5] The aggravation cited by expansionist politicians was a debt of

---

[4] "Exposición de motivos presentada por los Comisionados de México," in Antonio Peña y Reyes, *Algunos documentos sobre el Tratado de Guadalupe-Hidalgo y la situación de México durante la Invasion Americana* (México, D.F.: Porrúa, 1970), p. 160.

[5] John S.D. Eisenhower, *So Far from God; the U.S. War with Mexico, 1846-1848* (New York: Doubleday, 1989), p. xviii.

6,291,604.71 pesos, of which 2,026,139 had been paid off. The land was lost for the most part because Mexico had not succeeded in populating it, which calls up the great paradox that today it is Mexicans who have occupied it in great part.

For me, as a Mexican historian, the war presents an important question: how was it that the rich, prosperous New Spain, "the most precious jewel of the Spanish crown," had been converted in a few decades into the weak, impotent republic of 1846 and how, on the other hand the small Thirteen Colonies had been transformed into the ambitious, dynamic republic capable of snatching away half of the other's territory. It is undoubted that in 1783, when the Thirteen Colonies achieved independence, there was an imbalance in favor of the kingdom of New Spain, now Mexico (which until 1800 encompassed Louisiana, west of the Mississippi, ceded by France in 1763). The explanation of such a reverse is very complex.

The establishment of the United States was favored by many circumstances. The over half-century between the U.S. Declaration of Independence and the war of 1846-1848 was marked by blessings for them and misfortune for their southern neighbor. The independence of both grew out of the Seven Years War (1756-1763), in which Great Britain defeated France and Spain. Since all three ended up in bankruptcy, they tried to solve the problem by means of new taxes and by modernizing their governments. This generated bad feelings which led to independence. The British colonies broke off immediately, the Hispanic-American ones more slowly, because of the ties which bound them to the mother country and because they continued to prosper.

By way of further illustration, the priority given to rights and representation in the Anglo-American struggle assured sympathy for the colonists and that France and the Netherlands assisted them. The Thirteen Colonies were less important to Great Britain than her productive West Indies and so, with the French and Spanish alliance, it was assured that their war for independence would be short and not very bloody. Great Britain, with its government weak and diplomatically isolated, recognized U.S. independence in 1783, which allowed the United States to enter the concert of nations with full powers. Further, the United States was granted a generous frontier which included the part of Louisiana east of the Mississippi River, snatched away from France in 1762.

The establishment of the new nation involved difficulties, but a generation of brilliant politicians was able to overcome them; in 1789 having corrected the weaknesses of the first governmental experiment, that of the Confederacy, and having created a true unity by means of the federal constitution in 1789, it was just at that time when the French Revolution broke out and a quarter-century of European wars began. In this quarter-century the United States was able to experiment with its governance without external interference, to trade actively as a neutral nation, to absorb European immigration, to take advantage of Napoleon's offer in 1803 to buy Louisiana (returned to him by Spain in 1800), and to threaten the Spanish Floridas so that in 1817 Spain ceded the Floridas in exchange for a defined boundary between the United States and New Spain.

Thus, by the time Mexico became independent in 1821, the United States had doubled its territory and population, and the two countries had approximately the same extent of territory, although the northern neighbor already had a somewhat larger population. The great difference lay in the United States having a dynamic economy and a system of government which had become a model.

New Spain did not enjoy the same good fortune upon attaining independence. Her prosperity had begun to wither away at the end of the 18th century. The wars of the mother country had drained her of capital and the modernization of Spain had disrupted her society, government and economy, and the new taxes and monopolies had prompted bad times. The reorganization of the viceroyalty into intendencies, governed by a new "professional" bureaucracy, stripped away the powers of the former authorities and promoted divisions in the upper levels of government, on the eve of the profound imperial crisis which left Spain leaderless in 1808, when Napoleon invaded Spain and forced kings Charles IV and Ferdinand VII to turn the crown over to him. This juncture of events made it timely for the Spanish American colonies to begin their fight for independence.

But the case of New Spain was special, a fact that is generally forgotten: the kingdom retained a fundamental importance, not only for its own centers but also in an increasing way for Great Britain, France and the United States. New Spain's silver was essential for European business and warfare, in fact having been incorporated into the international marketplace. During the Napoleonic wars, silver from New Spain became a fundamental element for all the warring countries. This importance operated to endanger Mexico's drive for independence because it made her a target for the ambitions of commercial powers and of North American expansionists.

In keeping with the principles of the 19th century, Spanish bankruptcy had dragged New Spain down. All levels of society in this unfortunate ward of the mother country were oppressed with fiscal levies and voluntary loans, and as their revenues departed to the Caribbean or Europe, they were decapitalized. A decree in 1804 which confiscated the liquid capital of the church, which had served as banker for the country, left agriculture, mining and commerce without a source of credit. Because all classes of people were discontented, on the eve of independence, the old kingdom of New Spain was in crisis: indebted, stripped of capital, with the elite divided and the general population pauperized.

And Mexico did not possess the advantages of her neighbor to the north. The importance of the kingdom of New Spain for the empire made the fight for independence long and bloody. Furthermore she could not gain allies, as much because the European powers were focusing on halting Napoleonic expansion as because the excesses of the French Revolution had produced an atmosphere that did not welcome struggles for liberty.

Thus it was that the establishment of the new nation came about under deplorable conditions. The struggle had cost her the loss of half of the laboring class; her agriculture and commerce were in ruins; the mines were flooded, the highways full of thieves. Bankruptcy, under-capitalization, and political inexperience were feeble bases upon which to build a nation which covered an immense territory, lacking communications, and with a heterogeneous, poorly distributed population. All this, epitomized by her weakness before the commercial powers, made of Mexico the most threatened nation of the continent. First, she had to fight to liberate San Juan de Ulúa, occupied by the Spanish until 1825; then she faced the Spanish attempt at reconquest in 1829; afterwards the 1836 war with Texas, which became an international war because of the United States's involvement; in 1838, war with France, and in 1846-1848 the war with the United States. Even further, in the decade of the 1860s Mexico had to deal with a French intervention.

As an independent country, Mexico found herself entering into an unpropitious international stream of events. Recognition of her independence was difficult in a Europe frightened by libertarian movements and with a Great Alliance obsessed with "legitimism." Her former mother country continued to try to reconquer her with the help of the Holy Alliance, and did not recognize her independence until the end of 1836, forcing her to go into debt to defend herself.

The United States was regarded in the new nation with mixed feelings: admiration for her political system and development, and fear of her menacing expansionism. In order to obtain the desired progress, Mexico tried to imitate her, and Mexico's constitution was inspired by that of the United States. Because of the regionalism developed during the three centuries of the viceroyalty, however, the result was a federalism so radical that the resulting federal government was too weak to function successfully. The states were totally autonomous in fiscal matters and the federal government dependent upon customs receipts and upon quotas which the states were supposed to pay, proportionate to their prosperity and population. Because these quotas were paid irregularly, the government was reduced to dependence upon customs receipts and, in order to meet its extensive responsibilities, it was forced to borrow, and it fell into the embrace of speculators.

Mexico also tried to copy the colonization policy of the United States. As a reflection of her great hopes, Mexico offered greater inducements than the United States did in order to assure the loyalty of the colonists, but the results were disastrous. Although it has not been recognized, the Texans really did not have reasons for complaint as Andreas Reichstein has insisted in his book.[6] Perhaps this is the theme of North American history which requires most revision, since U.S. authors have repeated the arguments used to justify the Texan declaration of independence, a document designed to draw sympathy and assistance from the United States. In it are complaints of a non-existent tyranny, dictatorship and militarism and of not being able to practice their religion, "forgetting" that they had arrived as Catholics. The excuse of centralism, on the other hand, overlooked the fact that the first colonists had intrigued with centralist monarchists. Almost all of their complaints had been resolved by 1834, including the use of English in public business and the courts, and trial by jury.

In order to foment discontent, the annexationists worked on the colonists' fear of Mexican antislavery feeling and the resentment over the opening of a customs house, ending the extension of the period of exemption from import duties. Support from the United States was open and contradicted President Andrew Jackson's declaration of neutrality (debatable itself, for that matter, because the problem was a Mexican domestic matter). One careless slip by General Antonio López de Santa Anna at San Jacinto secured the independence of Texas, inasmuch as conditions in Mexico prevented the raising of another military expedition.

Although Jackson was not so bold as to annex Texas, before leaving office he extended recognition to the Republic of Texas, which contributed to the deterioration of relations between the United States and Mexico. This sums up the problem of the protests by citizens of Texas against the

---

[6] Andreas Reichstein, *The Rise of the Lone Star* (College Station: Texas A&M University Press, 1989).

Mexican government, much exaggerated or unjustified, which the United States agreed to submit to arbitration in 1838.

During the 1840s the imbalance of 1821 was accentuated. The population of the United States increased to more than twenty million, while that of Mexico was little more than seven million. Both countries confronted political factionalism and regional division, but the expansionist fever neutralized them in the United States, while to the south they made it difficult for any political system to function: federalism, centralism, and even temporary dictatorship were in effect between 1841 and 1843.

In 1845 a moderate government, aware of the impossibility of undertaking a war, started to negotiate with Texas. The failure of its efforts to annex Texas brought about its fall from power. At the end of the year, a totally bankrupt Mexico confronted two powerful dangers: war with the United States and a Spanish conspiracy to establish a monarchy. The country lacked allies, since Great Britain limited herself to urging that Mexico should avoid provoking hostilities, so that the United States would not have a pretext to take over the areas they desired.

But President Polk, even though he would have preferred to avoid a war by means of bribery or a simple purchase, was concluding to risk it in order to acquire California and New Mexico. He pretended then to engage in negotiation, but to stir things up he sent a commissioner with unsuitable credentials and offers of purchase. Mexico could not receive him. Upon arrival of news of this refusal by the Mexican government on January 13, 1846, Polk ordered General Zachary Taylor to advance to the Río Grande, into Mexican territory or, in the worst of cases, disputed territory. Eisenhower in his book observes that the communication to Taylor was composed very carefully to avoid any semblance of a declaration of war. Taylor was empowered to determine the moment when there would exist a "state of war" and to take the offensive when he determined it necessary, which for him was unconstitutional and clearly a measure taken behind the back of Winfield Scott, commanding general of the U.S. Army.

Upon reaching the bank of the Río Grande del Norte, in an exchange between representatives of the two armies, he was informed that he was in Mexican territory which was an act of war; the invaders replied that it was Texan territory and they were there to protect it. The presence of enemies in one's own land was sure to bring about some incident, such as took place in April. Taylor informed Polk in a succinct message that hostilities could be considered to have begun.

The message for declaring war was already prepared when Polk received Taylor's communication. Even though Mexico had been suffering aggression by the United States including assistance to the Texans, the incursion of General Edmund P. Gaines into Texas in 1836, the occupation of the port of Monterey in California in 1842, and the annexation of Texas, Polk cynically asserted:

> The grievous wrongs perpetrated by Mexico upon our citizens throughout a long period of years remain unredressed; and solemn treaties, pledging her public faith for this redress, have been disregarded ... . [W]e have tried every effort at reconciliation. The cup of forbearance had been exhausted, even before the recent information from the frontier of the Del Norte. But now, after reiterated menaces, Mexico has passed the boundary of the United States, has

invaded our territory, and shed American blood upon American soil. She has proclaimed that hostilities have commenced [?], and that the two nations are now at war.[7]

This message was sent to congress on May 12, 1846. Whig members of congress objected to assigning guilt to Mexico but, fearing to be considered "doves," they approved the president's calls for financial appropriations and manpower for war. The Mexican government did not declare war, but on July 7 congress declared that "a state of war exists."

Polk's administration was ready for war. Orders went out immediately for the Pacific and Gulf of Mexico fleets to blockade the main Mexican seaports. The secretary of war sent instructions to Colonel Stephen W. Kearny, at Fort Leavenworth in Missouri, to advance on New Mexico and California; to General John Wool to march with another army into Nuevo León, Coahuila and Chihuahua; and to Taylor to continue his advance into the interior of Mexico. Later another army was created to follow "the route of Cortez," from Veracruz to Mexico City.

Before Polk had formally declared war, the first battles had taken place on May 8 and 9 at Palo Alto and Resaca de la Palma. The Mexican disasters were foreseeable. North American historians have insisted that the U.S. Army was smaller than that of Mexico, but it is difficult to compare them by any reckoning. In the first place, the North Americans were able to dispatch several armies simultaneously to several fronts, while the navy blockaded Mexican ports, depriving the Mexican government of its main source of finances. Even given that the invading army might be small, its troops were trained and disciplined and commanded by professionals, possessing good organization and modern weapons. Because they had an unlimited power to mobilize volunteers, they could rotate the troops periodically. The government had the means to supply the army with everything necessary and to pay the soldiers. Even though they did not have plans or maps, and were unfamiliar with the terrain, their expert officers could make rapid reconnaissances and choose suitable locations for battles.

The Mexican army consisted of some 30,000 men, which was not enough to defend territory which extended from Oregon to Guatemala. The army was far from being professional and the majority of its volunteers, nearly always lacking training, fled at the first opportunity on the field of battle. Mexican bankruptcy had prevented modernizing the army's armament and this applied to the purchase of adequate munitions for the weapons they had, and even to get these they had to depend on profiteers who demanded exorbitant prices. The hundreds of women who fed and cared for the men assuredly added to the size of the army. On the other hand, even though the greater part of the Mexican army was located in the north, it was dispersed over the country, and the part that faced Taylor had to do the same later against Scott. Mexico needed a navy, but the two warships acquired in 1841 were sold to Great Britain on the eve of the war so that they would not fall into U.S. possession.

---

[7] James K. Polk to the Senate and House of Representatives. Washington, DC, May 12, 1846. James Richardson, ed., *A Compilation of the Messages and Papers of the Presidents, 1789-1906* (Washington, U.S. Congress, 1906), Vol. IV, pp. 441-492.

The greatest advantage of the invading army was its modern "flying" artillery, which determined the result of battles from the beginning. What is surprising is that, with antiquated short-range artillery, the Mexican Army was able to drive the North American army back at Angostura [Buena Vista].

Thus, as the war proceeded, the result was predictable and the North Americans knew it. Mexican politicians feared it, but the first defeats surprised the people and discredited centralism with the result that, in the middle of the war, federalism was reestablished. This radicalism was a new obstacle, not only in weakening the federal government which was left without fiscal resources, in spite of which all responsibility for the defense fell upon the national government, never mind that the changes of leaders and system of government distracted attention from the war.

Having a scanty population and being undefended, New Mexico and California were occupied with little difficulty, the central government being unable to help them. The conquest of New Mexico and California had been completed by January 1847. In other areas, the sacrifices of defenders were useless. The North Americans did not understand how, in spite of their defeats, Mexicans refused to make peace, and continued to improvise new armies to meet the invaders. At any rate, a starving army, poorly armed and unpaid, which witnessed the abandonment of the wounded and had to march to the north and to the west, to confront renewed enemy forces, was naturally demoralized.

The worst thing was that weakness amplified the political differences and prevented Mexicans from presenting a united front against the invasion. Some state governments thought they ought to conserve their resources against whatever danger, without understanding that the North American objective was "the halls of the Montezumas."

By August 1847 the invaders were in the Valley of Mexico and began to advance on the city from the south. Santa Anna negotiated an armistice in order to gain time, and named three commissioners to hear the proposals for a peace treaty presented by the U.S. commissioner, Nicholas Trist, who had been with Scott's army since May. The Mexican commissioners were not accorded powers to negotiate and, furthermore, they thought the North American propositions were extravagant. On September 8 hostilities were renewed. Following three defeats at the gates of Mexico City, the invaders occupied the capital on the 14th. Convinced of the impossibility of defending the city, the Mexican Army evacuated it. The city government negotiated with Scott for a peaceful entrance of the U.S. troops, but when the populace saw the North Americans entering they tried to defend the city and, with stones, knives and boiling water, they inflicted many casualties upon the invaders. Rivers of blood resulted, however, given the difference between the weapons of the soldiers and those of the civilians.

It was all useless and the flag bearing stars and stripes was raised over the National Palace by nightfall of the 15th. The North Americans celebrated their triumph noisily with liquor and music, while the Mexicans kept watch over their dead and Santa Anna, in the villa of Guadalupe Hidalgo, resigned the presidency and ordered the capital moved to Querétaro. The presidency devolved, under the constitution, on the president of the Supreme Court, Manuel de la Peña y Peña, who set out for Querétaro with some officials and the remains of the army.

In the United States, meanwhile, the military victories had stirred up a movement which called for taking over all of Mexico. Polk himself was planning to seize more territory "to punish the Mexicans" for prolonging the war.

The Moderates, led by De la Peña, concentrated on bringing congress together and getting leaders in the states to help organize the government. Trist communicated, through a British intermediary, his inclination to negotiate for peace. The Mexican government replied that they required only to assemble a quorum in congress in order to name Mexican commissioners. In November finally, Trist was informed that commissioners had been named: Luís Gonzaga Cuevas, Bernardo Couto, and Miguel Atristáin. But just at that moment Polk's order arrived requiring Trist to return to Washington. Upon his informing the Mexican government of this, De la Peña, Scott and the British minister urged him to remain, since he had already commenced to negotiate with the Mexican government and the instability of that government made it unlikely that peace could be attained if he departed, given that many Mexicans wished to continue the fighting.

Trist was undecided for a week between Polk's order and his own desire to bring an unjust war to a close. Finally, on December 4, he informed the Briton:

> I am now resolved to carry home with me a Treaty of Peace, if the Mexican Government feel strong enough to venture upon making one on the basis, as regards to boundary of the project originally presented by me [in August] ... . I should not now make the offer but for my clear and perfect conviction on these three points. First, that peace is still the desire of my government. Secondly, that if the present opportunity not be seized at once, all chance for making a treaty at all, will be lost ... . Thirdly, that this is the utmost point by which the Mexican government can by any possibility venture ... .[8]

The responsibility that Trist took upon himself was enormous, because in this he was advising that he had to observe Polk's minimal conditions and that his disobedience was going to cost him dearly, and in fact it would cost him his diplomatic career and even some of the salary that he was due, which was not paid until 1870.

Because of problems with nominating the Mexican commissioners and with their instructions, serious negotiations did not begin until January 2, 1848, although during December boundary problems were discussed. The talks were not easy, requiring consultations, coming up against vagueness of the available maps and problems of translation. The negotiations were concluded by January 28, but the commissioners wished to send the treaty to Querétaro for the government to give its approval. Trist, conscious of his great responsibility, was impatient and threatened to leave if the treaty were not signed immediately.

Finally, on February 2, 1848, in the afternoon, the signing of the treaty was carried out in the villa of Guadalupe Hidalgo. We know about the scene from a letter by Mrs. Nicholas Trist in which she related later what her husband had told her:

---

[8] Trist to Edward Thornton, Dec. 4, 1847. William Manning, ed. *Diplomatic Correspondence of the United States* (Washington: Carnegie Endowment for International Peace, 1937), Vol. VIII, pp. 984-985.

Just as they were about to sign the treaty in the "sanctuary" to which they repaired for the purpose, one of the Mexicans, Don Bernardo Couto, remarked to him [Trist], "this must be a proud moment for you; no less proud for you than it is humiliating for us." To this Mr. Trist replied, "we are making peace, let that be our thought." But, said he to us in relating it, "Could those Mexicans have seen into my heart at that moment, they would have known that my feeling of shame as an American was far stronger than theirs could be as Mexicans. For though it would not have done for me to say so there, that was a thing for every right-minded American to be ashamed of, and I was of it. This had been my feeling at all our conferences and especially at moments when I had felt it necessary to insist upon things which they were averse to. Had my course at such moments been governed by my conscience as a man, and my sense of justice as an individual American, I should have yielded in every instance. Nothing prevented my doing so but the conviction that the treaty would then be one which there would be no chance for the acceptance of by our government. My object, through out was, not to obtain all I could, but on the contrary to make the treaty as little exacting as possible from Mexico, as was compatible with its being accepted at home. In this I was governed by two considerations: one was the iniquity of the war, as an abuse of power on our part; the other was that the more disadvantageous the treaty was made for Mexico, the stronger would be the ground of opposition to it in the Mexican Congress by the party who had boasted of its ability to frustrate any peace measures.[9]

The treaty fixed the new Mexican boundary in accordance with the 1847 Disturnell map (Article V). Articles III and IV related to the terms under which American troops would evacuate and occupied premises would be returned. The rights of Mexicans remaining in the conquered provinces were guaranteed in Articles VIII and IX. Article X referred to lands in Texas and was annulled by the U.S. Congress. The ninth, the only article favorable to Mexico, guaranteed that the U.S. government would restrain the incursions into Mexico of bellicose Indians "and when they could not prevent them, they would punish and teach a lesson to the invaders, furthermore requiring them to pay reparations." This article was a dead letter, since the U.S. government did not at all try to honor it and required that it be canceled in the Treaty of Mesilla [Gadsden Purchase Treaty] of 1853. That document also renewed the Treaty of Friendship and Commerce and settled the manner in which differences would be resolved which might be raised in the future.

Trist sent the treaty to Polk immediately, while in Mexico a council made up of two Mexicans and two North Americans agreed upon a cessation of hostilities and the suspension, from the first of March, of the collection of war taxes by which the United States had come to rely in maintaining the occupation and carrying on the war.

Thanks also to the armistice it became possible to hold elections to congress in the occupied areas, necessary for congress to assemble to approve the treaty. The Moderates worked very hard to win in the elections because they knew that the Puros opposed the treaty and the Monarchists were organizing a movement to overthrow the Querétaro government. Several states tried to form a coalition to disavow the treaty and the government.

---

[9] Robert W. Drexler, *Guilty of Making Peace. A Biography of Nicholas P. Trist* (Lanham, London, New York: University Press of America, 1991), pp. 130-131.

The senators and deputies began to arrive in Querétaro at the end of April and finally, on May 7, a quorum was attained for convening congress, before which President De la Peña presented the treaty, the terms of which, until then, had been known only to the government and the commissioners. In his address he underlined the conditions under which the government had taken office and by which Mexican nationhood had been preserved without further compromises.

The Monarchist movement of Paredes fell apart and the Moderate majority was able to ratify the treaty. On May 26 the exchange of ratifications took place with senators Nathan Clifford and Ambrose H. Sevier, sent from the United States for this purpose. The states voted for a new president under the constitution, with the resulting election of José Joaquín de Herrera, who was able to reach Mexico City in June.

Mexicans regard the Treaty of Guadalupe Hidalgo as a very unhappy historical fact which we have to accept. On the negative side it stands for the loss of territory and citizens living therein. But it also has positive aspects which are not always stated. Mexico had been totally defeated and was at the point of disappearing or losing still more territory. Thanks being that Polk "made a mistake" in choosing an honest North American as commissioner, that did not happen. Nicholas Trist cherished truly democratic ideals and the Mexican commissioners, in their *Exposición de Motivos,* gave full credit to Mr. Trist's good qualities.[10] His good will made it possible for Baja California to be preserved and connected by land to Sonora. In addition, the damage to morale that the treaty signified to Mexicans made it possible for the different parties to begin to refine their national programs, so that with the entrance onto the scene of a new generation of Mexicans who were not bound to the colonial past, the Mexican nation would be consolidated. But the war and the treaty also operated to extend the feeling of nationality to most of the population and this brought to consciousness the importance of unity. Thus, facing the French menace in the 1860s, the attitude of the Mexican people would be different.

I believe that it would be appropriate for North Americans to accept the extent of their historic guilt in the event, so that they would abandon the anti-Mexican prejudices by which the war was justified, which manifest the old racism which it is also time to discard. Historically and geographically we are condemned to live alongside each other, which makes it essential that we should live together as we are humans, equals, though different. The rejection of Mexicans who, just as in an earlier time the poor colonists were coming to Texas and were accepted by Mexico, are migrating in search of a better life, and the work which they do to give reality to their dream, they contribute like all immigrants from all parts of the world, in order for the United States to maintain the dynamism which has always characterized it.

---

[10] "Permítamos Vuestra Excelencia manifestarle antes de concluir, que el buen concepto que en la primera negociación se formó del noble carácter y altas prendas del señor Trist, se ha confirmado cumplidamente en esta segunda. Dicha ha sido para ambos países que el Gobierno americano hubiese fijado su elección en persona tan digna, en amigo tan leal y sincero de la paz: de él no quedan en México sino recuerdos gratos y honrosos". *Exposición de motivos presentada por los Comisionados, p. 168.*

APPENDIX

Sobre la indemnización pecunaria que se ha convenido en el artículo XII 7 siguientes, son indispensables algunas explicaciones. Nosotros ofendaríamos el sentido común si no empeñásemos en demostrar que esa indemnización no es precio de la población de los territorios cedidos, porque ningún hombre de sano juicio podrá figurarse (especialmente después de vistos los artículos VIII 7 IX) que el Gobierno Mexicano ha entendido vender, y que el de los Estados Unidos ha pretendido comprar hombres ... . Pero debemos protestar que la dicha indemnización tampoco es precio de los territorios que quedaban para lo secesivo fuera de nuestra lína. Esos territorios no han sido vendidos en el Tratado; se habían perdido en la guerra; ésta ha marcado ahora con la espada los límites entre los Estados Unidos en México ... . Son la indemnización más alta que pudimos obtener como resarcimiento de los daños que resiente la República. Disminuída está por el acrecentamiento que en territorio adquiere su vecina, van a pesar sobre menor número de habitantes y sobre un pueblo menos grande, las mismas obligaciones que antes tenía, y por consiguiente son ya más satisfacerse exclusivamente de la porción del pueblo mexicano que conserva este nombre, cuando sin la cesión derramaría sobre la República toda tal como era antes. Daños de esa especie son los que en la parte posible se reparan con la indemnización.

INDEX